C-1553   CAREER EXAMINATION SERIES

This is your
PASSBOOK for...

Administrative Staff Analyst

Test Preparation Study Guide
Questions & Answers

COPYRIGHT NOTICE

This book is SOLELY intended for, is sold ONLY to, and its use is RESTRICTED to individual, bona fide applicants or candidates who qualify by virtue of having seriously filed applications for appropriate license, certificate, professional and/or promotional advancement, higher school matriculation, scholarship, or other legitimate requirements of education and/or governmental authorities.

This book is NOT intended for use, class instruction, tutoring, training, duplication, copying, reprinting, excerption, or adaptation, etc., by:

1) Other publishers
2) Proprietors and/or Instructors of "Coaching" and/or Preparatory Courses
3) Personnel and/or Training Divisions of commercial, industrial, and governmental organizations
4) Schools, colleges, or universities and/or their departments and staffs, including teachers and other personnel
5) Testing Agencies or Bureaus
6) Study groups which seek by the purchase of a single volume to copy and/or duplicate and/or adapt this material for use by the group as a whole without having purchased individual volumes for each of the members of the group
7) Et al.

Such persons would be in violation of appropriate Federal and State statutes.

PROVISION OF LICENSING AGREEMENTS – Recognized educational, commercial, industrial, and governmental institutions and organizations, and others legitimately engaged in educational pursuits, including training, testing, and measurement activities, may address request for a licensing agreement to the copyright owners, who will determine whether, and under what conditions, including fees and charges, the materials in this book may be used them. In other words, a licensing facility exists for the legitimate use of the material in this book on other than an individual basis. However, it is asseverated and affirmed here that the material in this book CANNOT be used without the receipt of the express permission of such a licensing agreement from the Publishers. Inquiries re licensing should be addressed to the company, attention rights and permissions department.

All rights reserved, including the right of reproduction in whole or in part, in any form or by any means, electronic or mechanical, including photocopying, recording, or by any information storage and retrieval system, without permission in writing from the Publisher.

Copyright © 2024 by
National Learning Corporation

212 Michael Drive, Syosset, NY 11791
(516) 921-8888 • www.passbooks.com
E-mail: info@passbooks.com

PUBLISHED IN THE UNITED STATES OF AMERICA

PASSBOOK® SERIES

THE *PASSBOOK® SERIES* has been created to prepare applicants and candidates for the ultimate academic battlefield – the examination room.

At some time in our lives, each and every one of us may be required to take an examination – for validation, matriculation, admission, qualification, registration, certification, or licensure.

Based on the assumption that every applicant or candidate has met the basic formal educational standards, has taken the required number of courses, and read the necessary texts, the *PASSBOOK® SERIES* furnishes the one special preparation which may assure passing with confidence, instead of failing with insecurity. Examination questions – together with answers – are furnished as the basic vehicle for study so that the mysteries of the examination and its compounding difficulties may be eliminated or diminished by a sure method.

This book is meant to help you pass your examination provided that you qualify and are serious in your objective.

The entire field is reviewed through the huge store of content information which is succinctly presented through a provocative and challenging approach – the question-and-answer method.

A climate of success is established by furnishing the correct answers at the end of each test.

You soon learn to recognize types of questions, forms of questions, and patterns of questioning. You may even begin to anticipate expected outcomes.

You perceive that many questions are repeated or adapted so that you can gain acute insights, which may enable you to score many sure points.

You learn how to confront new questions, or types of questions, and to attack them confidently and work out the correct answers.

You note objectives and emphases, and recognize pitfalls and dangers, so that you may make positive educational adjustments.

Moreover, you are kept fully informed in relation to new concepts, methods, practices, and directions in the field.

You discover that you are actually taking the examination all the time: you are preparing for the examination by "taking" an examination, not by reading extraneous and/or supererogatory textbooks.

In short, this PASSBOOK®, used directedly, should be an important factor in helping you to pass your test.

ADMINISTRATIVE STAFF ANALYST

DUTIES

Performs administrative supervision over staff analysts in studies and implementation of work methods, procedures and improvements; does related work.

The following are typical assignments within this class of positions. All personnel perform related work: Under varying levels of managerial or executive direction, with varying degrees of latitude for independent initiative, judgment and decision, Administrative Staff Analysts manage difficult and responsible professional work in the areas of budget, organizational research and personnel administration; manage budget work and the conduct of highly complex economic research and studies; manage organizational research work in the conduct of highly difficult and complex surveys and studies of organizational and operating problems of great difficulty and complexity, which may require the use of exceptionally difficult quantitative analysis, cost analysis and other research techniques, and make recommendations to executive management to obtain optimum efficiency in the utilization of staff, machines, equipment and space; manage personnel work in such areas as personnel relations, recruitment, position classification, compensation, employee selection, employee benefits, management studies, workforce planning, EEO programs, performance evaluation, staff development, labor relations, and other related areas; determine the need for contractual services and work with the Agency Chief Contracting Officer to define the scope of such services, and to select and evaluate appropriate vendors; serve as deputy to the head of a division or unit and/or plan and manage the activities of one or more units or other subdivisions of professional and other staff; serve as agency budget officer; may be in full charge of an agency's organizational research activities; serve as agency personnel officer; or perform assignments equivalent to those described above.

SCOPE OF THE EXAMINATION

The written test will be of the multiple-choice type and may include questions on supervision, managerial judgment, decisiveness and sensitivity; reading comprehension; written communication skills; coordinating, monitoring control, delegating, assigning, scheduling, organizing and planning skills; employee counseling/conflict resolution; attention to detail; skill and ability to perform research and compile information; basic quantitative skills; and ability to act under pressure.

HOW TO TAKE A TEST

I. YOU MUST PASS AN EXAMINATION

A. *WHAT EVERY CANDIDATE SHOULD KNOW*

Examination applicants often ask us for help in preparing for the written test. What can I study in advance? What kinds of questions will be asked? How will the test be given? How will the papers be graded?

As an applicant for a civil service examination, you may be wondering about some of these things. Our purpose here is to suggest effective methods of advance study and to describe civil service examinations.

Your chances for success on this examination can be increased if you know how to prepare. Those "pre-examination jitters" can be reduced if you know what to expect. You can even experience an adventure in good citizenship if you know why civil service exams are given.

B. *WHY ARE CIVIL SERVICE EXAMINATIONS GIVEN?*

Civil service examinations are important to you in two ways. As a citizen, you want public jobs filled by employees who know how to do their work. As a job seeker, you want a fair chance to compete for that job on an equal footing with other candidates. The best-known means of accomplishing this two-fold goal is the competitive examination.

Exams are widely publicized throughout the nation. They may be administered for jobs in federal, state, city, municipal, town or village governments or agencies.

Any citizen may apply, with some limitations, such as the age or residence of applicants. Your experience and education may be reviewed to see whether you meet the requirements for the particular examination. When these requirements exist, they are reasonable and applied consistently to all applicants. Thus, a competitive examination may cause you some uneasiness now, but it is your privilege and safeguard.

C. *HOW ARE CIVIL SERVICE EXAMS DEVELOPED?*

Examinations are carefully written by trained technicians who are specialists in the field known as "psychological measurement," in consultation with recognized authorities in the field of work that the test will cover. These experts recommend the subject matter areas or skills to be tested; only those knowledges or skills important to your success on the job are included. The most reliable books and source materials available are used as references. Together, the experts and technicians judge the difficulty level of the questions.

Test technicians know how to phrase questions so that the problem is clearly stated. Their ethics do not permit "trick" or "catch" questions. Questions may have been tried out on sample groups, or subjected to statistical analysis, to determine their usefulness.

Written tests are often used in combination with performance tests, ratings of training and experience, and oral interviews. All of these measures combine to form the best-known means of finding the right person for the right job.

II. HOW TO PASS THE WRITTEN TEST

A. NATURE OF THE EXAMINATION

To prepare intelligently for civil service examinations, you should know how they differ from school examinations you have taken. In school you were assigned certain definite pages to read or subjects to cover. The examination questions were quite detailed and usually emphasized memory. Civil service exams, on the other hand, try to discover your present ability to perform the duties of a position, plus your potentiality to learn these duties. In other words, a civil service exam attempts to predict how successful you will be. Questions cover such a broad area that they cannot be as minute and detailed as school exam questions.

In the public service similar kinds of work, or positions, are grouped together in one "class." This process is known as *position-classification*. All the positions in a class are paid according to the salary range for that class. One class title covers all of these positions, and they are all tested by the same examination.

B. FOUR BASIC STEPS

1) Study the announcement

How, then, can you know what subjects to study? Our best answer is: "Learn as much as possible about the class of positions for which you've applied." The exam will test the knowledge, skills and abilities needed to do the work.

Your most valuable source of information about the position you want is the official exam announcement. This announcement lists the training and experience qualifications. Check these standards and apply only if you come reasonably close to meeting them.

The brief description of the position in the examination announcement offers some clues to the subjects which will be tested. Think about the job itself. Review the duties in your mind. Can you perform them, or are there some in which you are rusty? Fill in the blank spots in your preparation.

Many jurisdictions preview the written test in the exam announcement by including a section called "Knowledge and Abilities Required," "Scope of the Examination," or some similar heading. Here you will find out specifically what fields will be tested.

2) Review your own background

Once you learn in general what the position is all about, and what you need to know to do the work, ask yourself which subjects you already know fairly well and which need improvement. You may wonder whether to concentrate on improving your strong areas or on building some background in your fields of weakness. When the announcement has specified "some knowledge" or "considerable knowledge," or has used adjectives like "beginning principles of..." or "advanced ... methods," you can get a clue as to the number and difficulty of questions to be asked in any given field. More questions, and hence broader coverage, would be included for those subjects which are more important in the work. Now weigh your strengths and weaknesses against the job requirements and prepare accordingly.

3) Determine the level of the position

Another way to tell how intensively you should prepare is to understand the level of the job for which you are applying. Is it the entering level? In other words, is this the position in which beginners in a field of work are hired? Or is it an intermediate or advanced level? Sometimes this is indicated by such words as "Junior" or "Senior" in the class title. Other jurisdictions use Roman numerals to designate the level – Clerk I, Clerk II, for example. The word "Supervisor" sometimes appears in the title. If the level is not indicated by the title, check the description of duties. Will you be working under very close supervision, or will you have responsibility for independent decisions in this work?

4) Choose appropriate study materials

Now that you know the subjects to be examined and the relative amount of each subject to be covered, you can choose suitable study materials. For beginning level jobs, or even advanced ones, if you have a pronounced weakness in some aspect of your training, read a modern, standard textbook in that field. Be sure it is up to date and has general coverage. Such books are normally available at your library, and the librarian will be glad to help you locate one. For entry-level positions, questions of appropriate difficulty are chosen – neither highly advanced questions, nor those too simple. Such questions require careful thought but not advanced training.

If the position for which you are applying is technical or advanced, you will read more advanced, specialized material. If you are already familiar with the basic principles of your field, elementary textbooks would waste your time. Concentrate on advanced textbooks and technical periodicals. Think through the concepts and review difficult problems in your field.

These are all general sources. You can get more ideas on your own initiative, following these leads. For example, training manuals and publications of the government agency which employs workers in your field can be useful, particularly for technical and professional positions. A letter or visit to the government department involved may result in more specific study suggestions, and certainly will provide you with a more definite idea of the exact nature of the position you are seeking.

III. KINDS OF TESTS

Tests are used for purposes other than measuring knowledge and ability to perform specified duties. For some positions, it is equally important to test ability to make adjustments to new situations or to profit from training. In others, basic mental abilities not dependent on information are essential. Questions which test these things may not appear as pertinent to the duties of the position as those which test for knowledge and information. Yet they are often highly important parts of a fair examination. For very general questions, it is almost impossible to help you direct your study efforts. What we can do is to point out some of the more common of these general abilities needed in public service positions and describe some typical questions.

1) General information

Broad, general information has been found useful for predicting job success in some kinds of work. This is tested in a variety of ways, from vocabulary lists to questions about current events. Basic background in some field of work, such as sociology or economics, may be sampled in a group of questions. Often these are principles which have become familiar to most persons through exposure rather than through formal training. It is difficult to advise you how to study for these questions; being alert to the world around you is our best suggestion.

2) Verbal ability

An example of an ability needed in many positions is verbal or language ability. Verbal ability is, in brief, the ability to use and understand words. Vocabulary and grammar tests are typical measures of this ability. Reading comprehension or paragraph interpretation questions are common in many kinds of civil service tests. You are given a paragraph of written material and asked to find its central meaning.

3) Numerical ability
Number skills can be tested by the familiar arithmetic problem, by checking paired lists of numbers to see which are alike and which are different, or by interpreting charts and graphs. In the latter test, a graph may be printed in the test booklet which you are asked to use as the basis for answering questions.

4) Observation
A popular test for law-enforcement positions is the observation test. A picture is shown to you for several minutes, then taken away. Questions about the picture test your ability to observe both details and larger elements.

5) Following directions
In many positions in the public service, the employee must be able to carry out written instructions dependably and accurately. You may be given a chart with several columns, each column listing a variety of information. The questions require you to carry out directions involving the information given in the chart.

6) Skills and aptitudes
Performance tests effectively measure some manual skills and aptitudes. When the skill is one in which you are trained, such as typing or shorthand, you can practice. These tests are often very much like those given in business school or high school courses. For many of the other skills and aptitudes, however, no short-time preparation can be made. Skills and abilities natural to you or that you have developed throughout your lifetime are being tested.

Many of the general questions just described provide all the data needed to answer the questions and ask you to use your reasoning ability to find the answers. Your best preparation for these tests, as well as for tests of facts and ideas, is to be at your physical and mental best. You, no doubt, have your own methods of getting into an exam-taking mood and keeping "in shape." The next section lists some ideas on this subject.

IV. KINDS OF QUESTIONS

Only rarely is the "essay" question, which you answer in narrative form, used in civil service tests. Civil service tests are usually of the short-answer type. Full instructions for answering these questions will be given to you at the examination. But in case this is your first experience with short-answer questions and separate answer sheets, here is what you need to know:

1) Multiple-choice Questions
Most popular of the short-answer questions is the "multiple choice" or "best answer" question. It can be used, for example, to test for factual knowledge, ability to solve problems or judgment in meeting situations found at work.
A multiple-choice question is normally one of three types—
- It can begin with an incomplete statement followed by several possible endings. You are to find the one ending which *best* completes the statement, although some of the others may not be entirely wrong.
- It can also be a complete statement in the form of a question which is answered by choosing one of the statements listed.

- It can be in the form of a problem – again you select the best answer.

Here is an example of a multiple-choice question with a discussion which should give you some clues as to the method for choosing the right answer:

When an employee has a complaint about his assignment, the action which will *best* help him overcome his difficulty is to
   A. discuss his difficulty with his coworkers
   B. take the problem to the head of the organization
   C. take the problem to the person who gave him the assignment
   D. say nothing to anyone about his complaint

In answering this question, you should study each of the choices to find which is best. Consider choice "A" – Certainly an employee may discuss his complaint with fellow employees, but no change or improvement can result, and the complaint remains unresolved. Choice "B" is a poor choice since the head of the organization probably does not know what assignment you have been given, and taking your problem to him is known as "going over the head" of the supervisor. The supervisor, or person who made the assignment, is the person who can clarify it or correct any injustice. Choice "C" is, therefore, correct. To say nothing, as in choice "D," is unwise. Supervisors have and interest in knowing the problems employees are facing, and the employee is seeking a solution to his problem.

2) True/False Questions

The "true/false" or "right/wrong" form of question is sometimes used. Here a complete statement is given. Your job is to decide whether the statement is right or wrong.

SAMPLE: A roaming cell-phone call to a nearby city costs less than a non-roaming call to a distant city.

This statement is wrong, or false, since roaming calls are more expensive.

This is not a complete list of all possible question forms, although most of the others are variations of these common types. You will always get complete directions for answering questions. Be sure you understand *how* to mark your answers – ask questions until you do.

V. RECORDING YOUR ANSWERS

Computer terminals are used more and more today for many different kinds of exams.
For an examination with very few applicants, you may be told to record your answers in the test booklet itself. Separate answer sheets are much more common. If this separate answer sheet is to be scored by machine – and this is often the case – it is highly important that you mark your answers correctly in order to get credit.

An electronic scoring machine is often used in civil service offices because of the speed with which papers can be scored. Machine-scored answer sheets must be marked with a pencil, which will be given to you. This pencil has a high graphite content which responds to the electronic scoring machine. As a matter of fact, stray dots may register as answers, so do not let your pencil rest on the answer sheet while you are pondering the correct answer. Also, if your pencil lead breaks or is otherwise defective, ask for another.

Since the answer sheet will be dropped in a slot in the scoring machine, be careful not to bend the corners or get the paper crumpled.

The answer sheet normally has five vertical columns of numbers, with 30 numbers to a column. These numbers correspond to the question numbers in your test booklet. After each number, going across the page are four or five pairs of dotted lines. These short dotted lines have small letters or numbers above them. The first two pairs may also have a "T" or "F" above the letters. This indicates that the first two pairs only are to be used if the questions are of the true-false type. If the questions are multiple choice, disregard the "T" and "F" and pay attention only to the small letters or numbers.

Answer your questions in the manner of the sample that follows:

32. The largest city in the United States is
    A. Washington, D.C.
    B. New York City
    C. Chicago
    D. Detroit
    E. San Francisco

1) Choose the answer you think is best. (New York City is the largest, so "B" is correct.)
2) Find the row of dotted lines numbered the same as the question you are answering. (Find row number 32)
3) Find the pair of dotted lines corresponding to the answer. (Find the pair of lines under the mark "B.")
4) Make a solid black mark between the dotted lines.

VI. BEFORE THE TEST

Common sense will help you find procedures to follow to get ready for an examination. Too many of us, however, overlook these sensible measures. Indeed, nervousness and fatigue have been found to be the most serious reasons why applicants fail to do their best on civil service tests. Here is a list of reminders:

- Begin your preparation early – Don't wait until the last minute to go scurrying around for books and materials or to find out what the position is all about.
- Prepare continuously – An hour a night for a week is better than an all-night cram session. This has been definitely established. What is more, a night a week for a month will return better dividends than crowding your study into a shorter period of time.
- Locate the place of the exam – You have been sent a notice telling you when and where to report for the examination. If the location is in a different town or otherwise unfamiliar to you, it would be well to inquire the best route and learn something about the building.
- Relax the night before the test – Allow your mind to rest. Do not study at all that night. Plan some mild recreation or diversion; then go to bed early and get a good night's sleep.
- Get up early enough to make a leisurely trip to the place for the test – This way unforeseen events, traffic snarls, unfamiliar buildings, etc. will not upset you.
- Dress comfortably – A written test is not a fashion show. You will be known by number and not by name, so wear something comfortable.

- Leave excess paraphernalia at home – Shopping bags and odd bundles will get in your way. You need bring only the items mentioned in the official notice you received; usually everything you need is provided. Do not bring reference books to the exam. They will only confuse those last minutes and be taken away from you when in the test room.
- Arrive somewhat ahead of time – If because of transportation schedules you must get there very early, bring a newspaper or magazine to take your mind off yourself while waiting.
- Locate the examination room – When you have found the proper room, you will be directed to the seat or part of the room where you will sit. Sometimes you are given a sheet of instructions to read while you are waiting. Do not fill out any forms until you are told to do so; just read them and be prepared.
- Relax and prepare to listen to the instructions
- If you have any physical problem that may keep you from doing your best, be sure to tell the test administrator. If you are sick or in poor health, you really cannot do your best on the exam. You can come back and take the test some other time.

VII. AT THE TEST

The day of the test is here and you have the test booklet in your hand. The temptation to get going is very strong. Caution! There is more to success than knowing the right answers. You must know how to identify your papers and understand variations in the type of short-answer question used in this particular examination. Follow these suggestions for maximum results from your efforts:

1) Cooperate with the monitor

The test administrator has a duty to create a situation in which you can be as much at ease as possible. He will give instructions, tell you when to begin, check to see that you are marking your answer sheet correctly, and so on. He is not there to guard you, although he will see that your competitors do not take unfair advantage. He wants to help you do your best.

2) Listen to all instructions

Don't jump the gun! Wait until you understand all directions. In most civil service tests you get more time than you need to answer the questions. So don't be in a hurry. Read each word of instructions until you clearly understand the meaning. Study the examples, listen to all announcements and follow directions. Ask questions if you do not understand what to do.

3) Identify your papers

Civil service exams are usually identified by number only. You will be assigned a number; you must not put your name on your test papers. Be sure to copy your number correctly. Since more than one exam may be given, copy your exact examination title.

4) Plan your time

Unless you are told that a test is a "speed" or "rate of work" test, speed itself is usually not important. Time enough to answer all the questions will be provided, but this does not mean that you have all day. An overall time limit has been set. Divide the total time (in minutes) by the number of questions to determine the approximate time you have for each question.

5) Do not linger over difficult questions

If you come across a difficult question, mark it with a paper clip (useful to have along) and come back to it when you have been through the booklet. One caution if you do this – be sure to skip a number on your answer sheet as well. Check often to be sure that you have not lost your place and that you are marking in the row numbered the same as the question you are answering.

6) Read the questions

Be sure you know what the question asks! Many capable people are unsuccessful because they failed to *read* the questions correctly.

7) Answer all questions

Unless you have been instructed that a penalty will be deducted for incorrect answers, it is better to guess than to omit a question.

8) Speed tests

It is often better NOT to guess on speed tests. It has been found that on timed tests people are tempted to spend the last few seconds before time is called in marking answers at random – without even reading them – in the hope of picking up a few extra points. To discourage this practice, the instructions may warn you that your score will be "corrected" for guessing. That is, a penalty will be applied. The incorrect answers will be deducted from the correct ones, or some other penalty formula will be used.

9) Review your answers

If you finish before time is called, go back to the questions you guessed or omitted to give them further thought. Review other answers if you have time.

10) Return your test materials

If you are ready to leave before others have finished or time is called, take ALL your materials to the monitor and leave quietly. Never take any test material with you. The monitor can discover whose papers are not complete, and taking a test booklet may be grounds for disqualification.

VIII. EXAMINATION TECHNIQUES

1) Read the general instructions carefully. These are usually printed on the first page of the exam booklet. As a rule, these instructions refer to the timing of the examination; the fact that you should not start work until the signal and must stop work at a signal, etc. If there are any *special* instructions, such as a choice of questions to be answered, make sure that you note this instruction carefully.

2) When you are ready to start work on the examination, that is as soon as the signal has been given, read the instructions to each question booklet, underline any key words or phrases, such as *least, best, outline, describe* and the like. In this way you will tend to answer as requested rather than discover on reviewing your paper that you *listed without describing*, that you selected the *worst* choice rather than the *best* choice, etc.

3) If the examination is of the objective or multiple-choice type – that is, each question will also give a series of possible answers: A, B, C or D, and you are called upon to select the best answer and write the letter next to that answer on your answer paper – it is advisable to start answering each question in turn. There may be anywhere from 50 to 100 such questions in the three or four hours allotted and you can see how much time would be taken if you read through all the questions before beginning to answer any. Furthermore, if you come across a question or group of questions which you know would be difficult to answer, it would undoubtedly affect your handling of all the other questions.

4) If the examination is of the essay type and contains but a few questions, it is a moot point as to whether you should read all the questions before starting to answer any one. Of course, if you are given a choice – say five out of seven and the like – then it is essential to read all the questions so you can eliminate the two that are most difficult. If, however, you are asked to answer all the questions, there may be danger in trying to answer the easiest one first because you may find that you will spend too much time on it. The best technique is to answer the first question, then proceed to the second, etc.

5) Time your answers. Before the exam begins, write down the time it started, then add the time allowed for the examination and write down the time it must be completed, then divide the time available somewhat as follows:
   - If 3-1/2 hours are allowed, that would be 210 minutes. If you have 80 objective-type questions, that would be an average of 2-1/2 minutes per question. Allow yourself no more than 2 minutes per question, or a total of 160 minutes, which will permit about 50 minutes to review.
   - If for the time allotment of 210 minutes there are 7 essay questions to answer, that would average about 30 minutes a question. Give yourself only 25 minutes per question so that you have about 35 minutes to review.

6) The most important instruction is to *read each question* and make sure you know what is wanted. The second most important instruction is to *time yourself properly* so that you answer every question. The third most important instruction is to *answer every question*. Guess if you have to but include something for each question. Remember that you will receive no credit for a blank and will probably receive some credit if you write something in answer to an essay question. If you guess a letter – say "B" for a multiple-choice question – you may have guessed right. If you leave a blank as an answer to a multiple-choice question, the examiners may respect your feelings but it will not add a point to your score. Some exams may penalize you for wrong answers, so in such cases *only*, you may not want to guess unless you have some basis for your answer.

7) Suggestions
   a. Objective-type questions
      1. Examine the question booklet for proper sequence of pages and questions
      2. Read all instructions carefully
      3. Skip any question which seems too difficult; return to it after all other questions have been answered
      4. Apportion your time properly; do not spend too much time on any single question or group of questions

5. Note and underline key words – *all, most, fewest, least, best, worst, same, opposite,* etc.
6. Pay particular attention to negatives
7. Note unusual option, e.g., unduly long, short, complex, different or similar in content to the body of the question
8. Observe the use of "hedging" words – *probably, may, most likely,* etc.
9. Make sure that your answer is put next to the same number as the question
10. Do not second-guess unless you have good reason to believe the second answer is definitely more correct
11. Cross out original answer if you decide another answer is more accurate; do not erase until you are ready to hand your paper in
12. Answer all questions; guess unless instructed otherwise
13. Leave time for review

   b. Essay questions
      1. Read each question carefully
      2. Determine exactly what is wanted. Underline key words or phrases.
      3. Decide on outline or paragraph answer
      4. Include many different points and elements unless asked to develop any one or two points or elements
      5. Show impartiality by giving pros and cons unless directed to select one side only
      6. Make and write down any assumptions you find necessary to answer the questions
      7. Watch your English, grammar, punctuation and choice of words
      8. Time your answers; don't crowd material

8) Answering the essay question

Most essay questions can be answered by framing the specific response around several key words or ideas. Here are a few such key words or ideas:

M's: manpower, materials, methods, money, management
P's: purpose, program, policy, plan, procedure, practice, problems, pitfalls, personnel, public relations
   a. Six basic steps in handling problems:
      1. Preliminary plan and background development
      2. Collect information, data and facts
      3. Analyze and interpret information, data and facts
      4. Analyze and develop solutions as well as make recommendations
      5. Prepare report and sell recommendations
      6. Install recommendations and follow up effectiveness

   b. Pitfalls to avoid
      1. *Taking things for granted* – A statement of the situation does not necessarily imply that each of the elements is necessarily true; for example, a complaint may be invalid and biased so that all that can be taken for granted is that a complaint has been registered

2. *Considering only one side of a situation* – Wherever possible, indicate several alternatives and then point out the reasons you selected the best one
3. *Failing to indicate follow up* – Whenever your answer indicates action on your part, make certain that you will take proper follow-up action to see how successful your recommendations, procedures or actions turn out to be
4. *Taking too long in answering any single question* – Remember to time your answers properly

IX. AFTER THE TEST

Scoring procedures differ in detail among civil service jurisdictions although the general principles are the same. Whether the papers are hand-scored or graded by machine we have described, they are nearly always graded by number. That is, the person who marks the paper knows only the number – never the name – of the applicant. Not until all the papers have been graded will they be matched with names. If other tests, such as training and experience or oral interview ratings have been given, scores will be combined. Different parts of the examination usually have different weights. For example, the written test might count 60 percent of the final grade, and a rating of training and experience 40 percent. In many jurisdictions, veterans will have a certain number of points added to their grades.

After the final grade has been determined, the names are placed in grade order and an eligible list is established. There are various methods for resolving ties between those who get the same final grade – probably the most common is to place first the name of the person whose application was received first. Job offers are made from the eligible list in the order the names appear on it. You will be notified of your grade and your rank as soon as all these computations have been made. This will be done as rapidly as possible.

People who are found to meet the requirements in the announcement are called "eligibles." Their names are put on a list of eligible candidates. An eligible's chances of getting a job depend on how high he stands on this list and how fast agencies are filling jobs from the list.

When a job is to be filled from a list of eligibles, the agency asks for the names of people on the list of eligibles for that job. When the civil service commission receives this request, it sends to the agency the names of the three people highest on this list. Or, if the job to be filled has specialized requirements, the office sends the agency the names of the top three persons who meet these requirements from the general list.

The appointing officer makes a choice from among the three people whose names were sent to him. If the selected person accepts the appointment, the names of the others are put back on the list to be considered for future openings.

That is the rule in hiring from all kinds of eligible lists, whether they are for typist, carpenter, chemist, or something else. For every vacancy, the appointing officer has his choice of any one of the top three eligibles on the list. This explains why the person whose name is on top of the list sometimes does not get an appointment when some of the persons lower on the list do. If the appointing officer chooses the second or third eligible, the No. 1 eligible does not get a job at once, but stays on the list until he is appointed or the list is terminated.

X. HOW TO PASS THE INTERVIEW TEST

The examination for which you applied requires an oral interview test. You have already taken the written test and you are now being called for the interview test – the final part of the formal examination.

You may think that it is not possible to prepare for an interview test and that there are no procedures to follow during an interview. Our purpose is to point out some things you can do in advance that will help you and some good rules to follow and pitfalls to avoid while you are being interviewed.

What is an interview supposed to test?

The written examination is designed to test the technical knowledge and competence of the candidate; the oral is designed to evaluate intangible qualities, not readily measured otherwise, and to establish a list showing the relative fitness of each candidate – as measured against his competitors – for the position sought. Scoring is not on the basis of "right" and "wrong," but on a sliding scale of values ranging from "not passable" to "outstanding." As a matter of fact, it is possible to achieve a relatively low score without a single "incorrect" answer because of evident weakness in the qualities being measured.

Occasionally, an examination may consist entirely of an oral test – either an individual or a group oral. In such cases, information is sought concerning the technical knowledges and abilities of the candidate, since there has been no written examination for this purpose. More commonly, however, an oral test is used to supplement a written examination.

Who conducts interviews?

The composition of oral boards varies among different jurisdictions. In nearly all, a representative of the personnel department serves as chairman. One of the members of the board may be a representative of the department in which the candidate would work. In some cases, "outside experts" are used, and, frequently, a businessman or some other representative of the general public is asked to serve. Labor and management or other special groups may be represented. The aim is to secure the services of experts in the appropriate field.

However the board is composed, it is a good idea (and not at all improper or unethical) to ascertain in advance of the interview who the members are and what groups they represent. When you are introduced to them, you will have some idea of their backgrounds and interests, and at least you will not stutter and stammer over their names.

What should be done before the interview?

While knowledge about the board members is useful and takes some of the surprise element out of the interview, there is other preparation which is more substantive. It *is* possible to prepare for an oral interview – in several ways:

1) Keep a copy of your application and review it carefully before the interview

This may be the only document before the oral board, and the starting point of the interview. Know what education and experience you have listed there, and the sequence and dates of all of it. Sometimes the board will ask you to review the highlights of your experience for them; you should not have to hem and haw doing it.

2) Study the class specification and the examination announcement

Usually, the oral board has one or both of these to guide them. The qualities, characteristics or knowledges required by the position sought are stated in these documents. They offer valuable clues as to the nature of the oral interview. For example, if the job involves supervisory responsibilities, the announcement will usually indicate that knowledge of modern supervisory methods and the qualifications of the candidate as a supervisor will be tested. If so, you can expect such questions, frequently in the form of a hypothetical situation which you are expected to solve. NEVER go into an oral without knowledge of the duties and responsibilities of the job you seek.

3) Think through each qualification required

Try to visualize the kind of questions you would ask if you were a board member. How well could you answer them? Try especially to appraise your own knowledge and background in each area, *measured against the job sought*, and identify any areas in which you are weak. Be critical and realistic – do not flatter yourself.

4) Do some general reading in areas in which you feel you may be weak

For example, if the job involves supervision and your past experience has NOT, some general reading in supervisory methods and practices, particularly in the field of human relations, might be useful. Do NOT study agency procedures or detailed manuals. The oral board will be testing your understanding and capacity, not your memory.

5) Get a good night's sleep and watch your general health and mental attitude

You will want a clear head at the interview. Take care of a cold or any other minor ailment, and of course, no hangovers.

What should be done on the day of the interview?

Now comes the day of the interview itself. Give yourself plenty of time to get there. Plan to arrive somewhat ahead of the scheduled time, particularly if your appointment is in the fore part of the day. If a previous candidate fails to appear, the board might be ready for you a bit early. By early afternoon an oral board is almost invariably behind schedule if there are many candidates, and you may have to wait. Take along a book or magazine to read, or your application to review, but leave any extraneous material in the waiting room when you go in for your interview. In any event, relax and compose yourself.

The matter of dress is important. The board is forming impressions about you – from your experience, your manners, your attitude, and your appearance. Give your personal appearance careful attention. Dress your best, but not your flashiest. Choose conservative, appropriate clothing, and be sure it is immaculate. This is a business interview, and your appearance should indicate that you regard it as such. Besides, being well groomed and properly dressed will help boost your confidence.

Sooner or later, someone will call your name and escort you into the interview room. *This is it.* From here on you are on your own. It is too late for any more preparation. But remember, you asked for this opportunity to prove your fitness, and you are here because your request was granted.

What happens when you go in?

The usual sequence of events will be as follows: The clerk (who is often the board stenographer) will introduce you to the chairman of the oral board, who will introduce you to the other members of the board. Acknowledge the introductions before you sit down. Do not be surprised if you find a microphone facing you or a stenotypist sitting by. Oral interviews are usually recorded in the event of an appeal or other review.

Usually the chairman of the board will open the interview by reviewing the highlights of your education and work experience from your application – primarily for the benefit of the other members of the board, as well as to get the material into the record. Do not interrupt or comment unless there is an error or significant misinterpretation; if that is the case, do not hesitate. But do not quibble about insignificant matters. Also, he will usually ask you some question about your education, experience or your present job – partly to get you to start talking and to establish the interviewing "rapport." He may start the actual questioning, or turn it over to one of the other members. Frequently, each member undertakes the questioning on a particular area, one in which he is perhaps most competent, so you can expect each member to participate in the examination. Because time is limited, you may also expect some rather abrupt switches in the direction the questioning takes, so do not be upset by it. Normally, a board member will not pursue a single line of questioning unless he discovers a particular strength or weakness.

After each member has participated, the chairman will usually ask whether any member has any further questions, then will ask you if you have anything you wish to add. Unless you are expecting this question, it may floor you. Worse, it may start you off on an extended, extemporaneous speech. The board is not usually seeking more information. The question is principally to offer you a last opportunity to present further qualifications or to indicate that you have nothing to add. So, if you feel that a significant qualification or characteristic has been overlooked, it is proper to point it out in a sentence or so. Do not compliment the board on the thoroughness of their examination – they have been sketchy, and you know it. If you wish, merely say, "No thank you, I have nothing further to add." This is a point where you can "talk yourself out" of a good impression or fail to present an important bit of information. Remember, *you close the interview yourself*.

The chairman will then say, "That is all, Mr. _____, thank you." Do not be startled; the interview is over, and quicker than you think. Thank him, gather your belongings and take your leave. Save your sigh of relief for the other side of the door.

How to put your best foot forward

Throughout this entire process, you may feel that the board individually and collectively is trying to pierce your defenses, seek out your hidden weaknesses and embarrass and confuse you. Actually, this is not true. They are obliged to make an appraisal of your qualifications for the job you are seeking, and they want to see you in your best light. Remember, they must interview all candidates and a non-cooperative candidate may become a failure in spite of their best efforts to bring out his qualifications. Here are 15 suggestions that will help you:

1) Be natural – Keep your attitude confident, not cocky

If you are not confident that you can do the job, do not expect the board to be. Do not apologize for your weaknesses, try to bring out your strong points. The board is interested in a positive, not negative, presentation. Cockiness will antagonize any board member and make him wonder if you are covering up a weakness by a false show of strength.

2) Get comfortable, but don't lounge or sprawl

Sit erectly but not stiffly. A careless posture may lead the board to conclude that you are careless in other things, or at least that you are not impressed by the importance of the occasion. Either conclusion is natural, even if incorrect. Do not fuss with your clothing, a pencil or an ashtray. Your hands may occasionally be useful to emphasize a point; do not let them become a point of distraction.

3) Do not wisecrack or make small talk

This is a serious situation, and your attitude should show that you consider it as such. Further, the time of the board is limited – they do not want to waste it, and neither should you.

4) Do not exaggerate your experience or abilities

In the first place, from information in the application or other interviews and sources, the board may know more about you than you think. Secondly, you probably will not get away with it. An experienced board is rather adept at spotting such a situation, so do not take the chance.

5) If you know a board member, do not make a point of it, yet do not hide it

Certainly you are not fooling him, and probably not the other members of the board. Do not try to take advantage of your acquaintanceship – it will probably do you little good.

6) Do not dominate the interview

Let the board do that. They will give you the clues – do not assume that you have to do all the talking. Realize that the board has a number of questions to ask you, and do not try to take up all the interview time by showing off your extensive knowledge of the answer to the first one.

7) Be attentive

You only have 20 minutes or so, and you should keep your attention at its sharpest throughout. When a member is addressing a problem or question to you, give him your undivided attention. Address your reply principally to him, but do not exclude the other board members.

8) Do not interrupt

A board member may be stating a problem for you to analyze. He will ask you a question when the time comes. Let him state the problem, and wait for the question.

9) Make sure you understand the question

Do not try to answer until you are sure what the question is. If it is not clear, restate it in your own words or ask the board member to clarify it for you. However, do not haggle about minor elements.

10) Reply promptly but not hastily

A common entry on oral board rating sheets is "candidate responded readily," or "candidate hesitated in replies." Respond as promptly and quickly as you can, but do not jump to a hasty, ill-considered answer.

11) Do not be peremptory in your answers

A brief answer is proper – but do not fire your answer back. That is a losing game from your point of view. The board member can probably ask questions much faster than you can answer them.

12) Do not try to create the answer you think the board member wants

He is interested in what kind of mind you have and how it works – not in playing games. Furthermore, he can usually spot this practice and will actually grade you down on it.

13) Do not switch sides in your reply merely to agree with a board member

Frequently, a member will take a contrary position merely to draw you out and to see if you are willing and able to defend your point of view. Do not start a debate, yet do not surrender a good position. If a position is worth taking, it is worth defending.

14) Do not be afraid to admit an error in judgment if you are shown to be wrong

The board knows that you are forced to reply without any opportunity for careful consideration. Your answer may be demonstrably wrong. If so, admit it and get on with the interview.

15) Do not dwell at length on your present job

The opening question may relate to your present assignment. Answer the question but do not go into an extended discussion. You are being examined for a *new* job, not your present one. As a matter of fact, try to phrase ALL your answers in terms of the job for which you are being examined.

Basis of Rating

Probably you will forget most of these "do's" and "don'ts" when you walk into the oral interview room. Even remembering them all will not ensure you a passing grade. Perhaps you did not have the qualifications in the first place. But remembering them will help you to put your best foot forward, without treading on the toes of the board members.

Rumor and popular opinion to the contrary notwithstanding, an oral board wants you to make the best appearance possible. They know you are under pressure – but they also want to see how you respond to it as a guide to what your reaction would be under the pressures of the job you seek. They will be influenced by the degree of poise you display, the personal traits you show and the manner in which you respond.

ABOUT THIS BOOK

This book contains tests divided into Examination Sections. Go through each test, answering every question in the margin. We have also attached a sample answer sheet at the back of the book that can be removed and used. At the end of each test look at the answer key and check your answers. On the ones you got wrong, look at the right answer choice and learn. Do not fill in the answers first. Do not memorize the questions and answers, but understand the answer and principles involved. On your test, the questions will likely be different from the samples. Questions are changed and new ones added. If you understand these past questions you should have success with any changes that arise. Tests may consist of several types of questions. We have additional books on each subject should more study be advisable or necessary for you. Finally, the more you study, the better prepared you will be. This book is intended to be the last thing you study before you walk into the examination room. Prior study of relevant texts is also recommended. NLC publishes some of these in our Fundamental Series. Knowledge and good sense are important factors in passing your exam. Good luck also helps. So now study this Passbook, absorb the material contained within and take that knowledge into the examination. Then do your best to pass that exam.

EXAMINATION SECTION

EXAMINATION SECTION
TEST 1

DIRECTIONS: Each question or incomplete statement is followed by several suggested answers or completions. Select the one that BEST answers the question or completes the statement. *PRINT THE LETTER OF THE CORRECT ANSWER IN THE SPACE AT THE RIGHT.*

1. The one of the following which has had GREATEST effect upon size of the budget of large cities in the last twenty years is
   A. change in the organization of the city resulting from new charters
   B. increase in services rendered by the city
   C. development of independent authorities
   D. increase in the city's ability to borrow money
   E. increase in the size of the city

   1.____

2. The one of the following services for which cities receive the LEAST amount of direct financial assistance from state governments is
   A. education B. welfare C. housing
   D. roads E. museums

   2.____

3. Major problems which face most large cities, including New York, arise from the vertical sandwiching of governments in a single area and from the many independent governments that crowd the boundaries of the central city.
   Of the following methods of solving these problems, the one which has been MOST successful in the past has been to
   A. decentralize the administration of the central city
   B. create various supra-municipal authorities which tend to integrate the activities of the metropolitan area
   C. bring the metropolitan population under a single local government
   D. set up intermunicipal coordinating agencies to solve area administrative and economic problems
   E. allow each government element in the metropolitan area to work out its own solution

   3.____

4. By means of the *debt limit*, the states regulate many facets of the debt of the cities.
   The one of the following factors which is NOT regulated in this manner is the
   A. purpose for which the debt is incurred
   B. amount of debt which may be incurred
   C. terms of the notes or bonds issued by the city
   D. forms of debts which may be incurred
   E. source from which the money may be borrowed

   4.____

5. The one of the following which is a characteristic of NEITHER the state nor the federal governments, but which is a characteristic of the government of cities is that the latter
   A. is not sovereign but an agent
   B. does not have the power to raise taxes
   C. cannot enter into contracts
   D. may not make treaties with foreign countries
   E. may not coin money

5.____

Questions 6-8.

DIRECTIONS: Questions 6 through 8 are to be answered on the basis of the following paragraph.

The regressive uses of discipline is ubiquitous. Administrative architects who seek the optimum balance between structure and morale must accordingly look toward the identification and isolation of disciplinary elements. The whole range of disciplinary sanctions, from the reprimand to the dismissal presents opportunities for reciprocity and accommodation of institutional interests. When rightly seized upon, these opportunities may provide the moment and the means for fruitful exercise of leadership and collaboration.

6. The one of the following ways of reworking the ideas presented in this paragraph in order to be BEST suited for presentation in an in-service training course in supervision is:
   A. When one of your men does something wrong, talk it over with him. Tell him what he should have done. This is a chance for you to show the man that you are on his side and that you would welcome him on your side.
   B. It is not necessary to reprimand or to dismiss an employee because he needs disciplining. The alert foreman will lead and collaborate with his subordinates making discipline unnecessary.
   C. A good way to lead the men you supervise is to take those opportunities which present themselves to use the whole range of disciplinary sanctions from reprimand to dismissal as a means for enforcing collaboration.
   D. Chances to punish a man in your squad should be welcomed as opportunities to show that you are a "*good guy*" who does not bear a grudge.
   E. Before you talk to a man or have him report to the office for something he has done wrong, attempt to lead him and get him to work with you. Tell him that his actions were wrong, that you expect him not to repeat the same wrong act, and that you will take a firmer stand if the act is repeated.

6.____

7. Of the following, the PRINCIPAL point made in the paragraph is that
   A. discipline is frequently used improperly
   B. it is possible to isolate the factors entering into a disciplinary situation
   C. identification of the disciplinary elements is desirable

7.____

D. disciplinary situations may be used to the advantage of the organization
E. obtaining the best relationship between organizational form and spirit, depend upon the ability to label disciplinary elements

8. The MOST novel idea presented in the paragraph is that 8.____
   A. discipline is rarely necessary
   B. discipline may be a joint action of man and supervisor
   C. there are disciplinary elements which may be identified
   D. a range of disciplinary sanctions exist
   E. it is desirable to seek for balance between structure and morale

9. When, in the process of developing a classification plan, it has been decided that 9.____
   certain positions all have distinguishing characteristics sufficiently similar to justify treating them alike in the process of selecting appointees and establishing pay rates or scales, then the kind of employment represented by such positions will be called a "class."
   According to this paragraph, a group of positions is called a class if they
   A. have distinguishing characteristics
   B. represent a kind of employment
   C. can be treated in the same manner for some functions
   D. all have the same pay rates
   E. are treated in the same manner in the development of a classification plan

Questions 10-12.

DIRECTIONS: Questions 10 through 12 are to be answered on the basis of the following paragraph.

The fundamental characteristic of the type of remote control which management needs to bridge the gap between itself and actual operations is the more effective use of records and reports—more specifically, the gathering and interpretation of the facts contained in records and reports. Facts, for management purposes, are those data (narrative and quantitative) which express in simple terms the current standing of the agency's program, work and resources in relation to the plans and policies formulated by management. They are those facts or measures (1) which permit management to compare current status with past performance and with its forecasts for the immediate future, and (2) which provide management with a reliable basis for long-range forecasting.

10. According to the above statement, a characteristic of a type of management 10.____
    control
    A. is the kind of facts contained in records and reports
    B. is narrative and quantitative data
    C. is its remoteness from actual operations
    D. is the use of records
    E. which expresses in simple terms the current standing of the agency's program, provides management with a reliable basis for long-range forecasting

11. For management purposes, facts are, according to the paragraph,   11.____
    A. forecasts which can be compared to current status
    B. data which can be used for certain control purposes
    C. a fundamental characteristic of a type of remote control
    D. the data contained in records and reports
    E. data (narrative and quantitative) which describe the plans and policies formulated by management

12. An inference which can be drawn from this statement is that   12.____
    A. management which has a reliable basis for long-range forecasting has at its disposal a type of remote control which is needed to bridge the gap between itself and actual operations
    B. data which do not express in simple terms the current standing of the agency's program, work and resources in relationship to the plans and policies formulated by management, may still be facts for management purposes
    C. data which express relationships among the agency's program, work, and resources are management facts
    D. the gap between management and actual operations can only be bridged by characteristics which are fundamentally a type of remote control
    E. management compares current status with past performance in order to obtain a reliable basis for long-range forecasting

Questions 13-14.

DIRECTIONS: Questions 13 and 14 are to be answered on the basis of the following paragraph.

People must be selected to do the tasks involved and must be placed on a payroll in jobs fairly priced. Each of these people must be assigned those tasks which he can perform best: the work of each must be appraised, and good and poor work singled out appropriately. Skill in performing assigned tasks must be developed, and the total work situation must be conducive to sustained high performance. Finally, employees must be separated from the work force either voluntarily or involuntarily because of inefficient or unsatisfactory performance or because of curtailment of organizational activities.

13. A personnel function which is NOT included in the above description is   13.____
    A. classification   B. training   C. placement
    D. severance   E. service rating

14. The underlying implied purpose of the policy enunciated in the above paragraph is   14.____
    A. to plan for the curtailment of the organizational program when it becomes necessary
    B. to single out appropriate skill in performing assigned tasks
    C. to develop and maintain a high level of performance by employees

D. that training employees in relation to the total work situation is essential if good and poor work are to be singled out
E. that equal money for equal work results in a total work situation which insures proper appraisal

15. Changes in program must be quickly and effectively translated into organizational adjustments if the administrative machinery is to be fully adapted to current operating needs. Continuous administrative planning is indispensable to the successful and expeditious accomplishment of such organization changes. According to this statement, 15._____
    A. the absence of continuous administrative planning must result in out-moded administrative machinery
    B. continuous administrative planning is necessary for changes in program
    C. if changes in program are quickly and effectively translated into organizational adjustments, the administrative machinery is fully adapted to current operating needs
    D. continuous administrative planning results in successful and expeditious accomplishment of organization changes
    E. if administrative machinery is not fully adapted to current operating needs, then continuous administrative planning is absent

16. The first-line supervisor executes policy as elsewhere formulated. He does not make policy. He is the element of the administrative structure closest to the employee group.
    From this point of view, it follows that a MAJOR function of the first-line supervisor is to 16._____
    A. suggest desirable changes in procedure to top management
    B. prepare time schedules showing when his unit will complete a piece of work so that it will dovetail with the requirements of other units
    C. humanize policy so as to respect employee needs and interests
    D. report danger points to top management in order to forestall possible bottlenecks
    E. discipline employees who continuously break departmental rules

17. During a supervisory staff meeting, the department head said to the first-line supervisors, "*The most important job you have is to get across to the employees in your units the desirability of achieving our department's aims and the importance of the jobs they are performing toward reaching our goals.*"
    In general, adoption of this point of view would tend to result in an organization 17._____
    A. in which supervisors would be faced by many disciplinary problems caused by employee reaction to the program
    B. in which less supervision is required of the work of the average employee
    C. having more clearly defined avenues of communication
    D. lacking definition; supervisors would tend to forget their primary mission of getting the assigned work completed as efficiently as possible
    E. in which most employees would be capable of taking over a supervisory position when necessary

18. A supervisor, in assigning a man to a job, generally followed the policy of fitting the man to the job.
    This procedure is
    A. *undesirable*; the job should be fitted to the man
    B. *desirable*; primary emphasis should be on the work to be accomplished
    C. *undesirable*; the policy does not consider human values
    D. *desirable*; setting up a definite policy and following it permits careful analysis
    E. *undesirable*; it is not always possible to fit the available man to the job

19. Assume that one of the units under your jurisdiction has 40 typists. Their skill range from 15 to 80 words a minute.
    The MOST feasible of the following methods to increase the typing output of this unit is to
    A. study the various typing jobs to determine the skill requirements for each type of work and assign to each typist tasks commensurate with her skill
    B. assign the slow typists to clerical work and hire new typists
    C. assign such tasks as typing straight copy to the slower typists
    D. reduce the skill requirements necessary to produce a satisfactory quantity of work
    E. simplify procedures and keep records, memoranda, and letters short and concise

20. In a division of a department, private secretaries were assigned to members of the technical staff since each required a secretary who was familiar with his particular field and who could handle various routine matters without referring to anyone. Other members of the staff depended for their dictation and typing work upon a small pool consisting of two stenographers and two typists. Because of turnover and the difficulty of recruiting new stenographers and typists, the pool had to be discontinued.
    Of the following, the MOST satisfactory way to provide stenographic and typing service for the division is to
    A. organize the private secretaries into a decentralized pool under the direction of a supervisor to whom nontechnical staff members would send requests for stenographic and typing assistance
    B. organize the private secretaries into a central pool under the direction of a supervisor to whom all staff members would send requests for stenographic and typing assistance
    C. train clerks as typists and typists as stenographers
    D. relieve stenographers and typists of jobs that can be done by messengers or clerks
    E. conserve time by using such devices as indicating minor corrections on a final draft in such a way that they can be erased and by using duplicating machines to eliminate typing many copies

21. Even under perfect organizational conditions, the relationships between the line units and the units charged with budget planning and personnel management may be precarious at times.
The one of the following which is a MAJOR reason for this is that
    A. service units assist the head of the agency in formulating and executing policies
    B. line units frequently find lines of communication to the agency head blocked by service units
    C. there is a natural antagonism between planners and doers
    D. service units tend to become line in attitude and emphasis, and to conflict with operating units
    E. service units tend to function apart from the operating units

21.____

22. The one of the following which is the CHIEF reason for training supervisors is that
    A. untrained supervisors find it difficult to train their subordinates
    B. most persons do not start as supervisors and consequently are in need of supervisory training
    C. training permits a higher degree of decentralization of the decision-making process
    D. training permits a higher degree of centralization of the decision-making process
    E. coordinated actions on the part of many persons pre-supposes familiarity with the procedures to be employed

22.____

23. The problem of determining the type of organization which should exist is inextricably interwoven with the problem of recruitment.
In general, this statement is
    A. *correct*; since organizations are man-made, they can be changed
    B. *incorrect*; the organizational form which is most desirable is independent of the persons involved
    C. *correct*; the problem of organization cannot be considered apart from employee qualifications
    D. *incorrect*; organizational problems can be separated into many parts and recruitment is important in only few of these
    E. *correct*; a good recruitment program will reduce the problems of organization

23.____

24. The conference as an administrative tool is MOST valuable for solving problems which
    A. are simple and within a familiar frame of reference
    B. are of long standing
    C. are novel and complex
    D. are not solvable
    E. require immediate solution

24.____

25. Of the following, a recognized procedure for avoiding conflicts in the delegation of authority is to
    A. delegate authority so as to preserve control by top management
    B. provide for a workable span of control
    C. preview all assignments periodically
    D. assign all related work to the same control
    E. use the linear method of assignment

25.____

KEY (CORRECT ANSWERS)

1.	B		11.	B
2.	E		12.	A
3.	C		13.	A
4.	E		14.	C
5.	A		15.	A
6.	A		16.	C
7.	D		17.	B
8.	B		18.	B
9.	C		19.	A
10.	D		20.	A

21.	D
22.	C
23.	C
24.	C
25.	D

TEST 2

DIRECTIONS: Each question or incomplete statement is followed by several suggested answers or completions. Select the one that BEST answers the question or completes the statement. *PRINT THE LETTER OF THE CORRECT ANSWER IN THE SPACE AT THE RIGHT.*

1. A danger which exists in any organization as complex as that required for administration of a large city is that each department comes to believe that it exists for its own sake.
   The one of the following which has been attempted in some organizations as a cure for this condition is to
   A. build up the departmental esprit de corps
   B. expand the functions and jurisdictions of the various departments so that better integration is possible
   C. develop a body of specialists in the various subject matter fields which cut across departmental lines
   D. delegate authority to the lowest possible echelon
   E. systematically transfer administrative personnel from one department to another

   1.____

2. At best, the organization chart is ordinarily and necessarily an idealized picture of the intent of top management, a reflection of hopes and aims rather than a photograph of the operating facts within an organization.
   The one of the following which is the BASIC reason for this is that the organization chart
   A. does not show the flow of work within the organization
   B. speaks in terms of positions rather than of live employees
   C. frequently contains unresolved internal ambiguities
   D. is a record of past organization or of proposed future organization and never a photograph of the living organization
   E. does not label the jurisdiction assigned to each component unit

   2.____

3. The drag of inadequacy is always downward. The need in administration is always for the reverse; for a department head to project his thinking to the city level, for the unit chief to try to see the problems of the department.
   The inability of a city administration to recruit administrators who can satisfy this need usually results in departments characterized by
   A. disorganization   B. poor supervision
   C. circumscribed viewpoints D. poor public relations
   E. a lack of programs

   3.____

4. When, as a result of a shift in public sentiment, the elective officers of a city are changed, is it desirable for career administrators to shift ground without performing any illegal or dishonest act in order to conform to the policies of the new elective officers?
   A. *No;* the opinions and beliefs of the career officials are the result of long experience in administration and are more reliable than those of politicians.

   4.____

B. *Yes*; only in this way can citizens, political officials, and career administrators alike have confidence in the performance of their respective functions.
C. *No*; a top career official who is so spineless as to change his views or procedures as a result of public opinion is of little value to the public service.
D. *Yes*; legal or illegal, it is necessary that a city employee carry out the orders of his superior officers
E. *No*; shifting ground with every change in administration will preclude the use of a constant overall policy.

5. Participation in developing plans which will affect levels in the organization in addition to his own, will contribute to an individual's understanding of the entire system. When possible, this should be encouraged.
This policy is, in general,
    A. *desirable*; the maintenance of any organization depends upon individual understanding
    B. *undesirable*; employees should participate only in those activities which affect their own level, otherwise conflicts in authority may arise
    C. *desirable*; an employee's will to contribute to the maintenance of an organization depends to a great extent on the level which he occupies
    D. *undesirable*; employees can be trained more efficiently and economically in an organized training program than by participating in plan development
    E. *desirable*; it will enable the employee to make intelligent suggestions for adjustment of the plan in the future

5.____

6. Constant study should be made of the information contained in reports to isolate those elements of experience which are static, those which are variable and repetitive, and those which are variable and due to chance.
Knowledge of those elements of experience in his organization which are static or constant will enable the operating official to
    A. fix responsibility for their supervision at a lower level
    B. revise the procedure in order to make the elements variable
    C. arrange for follow-up and periodic adjustment
    D. bring related data together
    E. provide a frame of reference within which detailed standards for measure-meant can be installed

6.____

7. A chief staff officer, serving as one of the immediate advisors to the department head, has demonstrated a special capacity for achieving internal agreements and for sound judgment. As a result he has been used more and more as a source of counsel and assistance by the department head. Other staff officers and line officials as well have discovered that it is wise for them to check with this colleague in advance on all problematical matters handed up to the department head.
Developments such as this are
    A. *undesirable*; they disrupt the normal lines for flow of work in an organization

7.____

B. *desirable*; they allow an organization to make the most of its strength wherever such strength resides
C. *undesirable*; they tend to undermine the authority of the department head and put it in the hands of a staff officer who does not have the responsibility
D. *desirable*; they tend to resolve internal ambiguities in organization
E. *undesirable*; they make for bad morale by causing *cut throat* competition

8. A common difference among executives is that some are not content unless they are out in front of everything that concerns their organization, while others prefer to run things by pulling strings, by putting others out in front and by stepping into the breach only when necessary.
Generally speaking, an advantage this latter method of operation has over the former is that it
    A. results in a higher level of morale over a sustained period of time
    B. gets results by exhortation and direct stimulus
    C. makes it necessary to calculate integrated moves
    D. makes the personality of the executive felt further down the line
    E. results in the executive getting the reputation for being a good fellow

8.____

9. Administrators frequently have to get facts by interviewing people. Although the interview is a legitimate fact-gathering technique, it has definite limitations which should not be overlooked.
The one of the following which is an important limitation is that
    A. people who are interviewed frequently answer questions with guesses rather than admit their ignorance
    B. it is a poor way to discover the general attitude and thinking of supervisors interviewed
    C. people sometimes hesitate to give information during an interview which they will submit in written form
    D. it is a poor way to discover how well employees understand departmental policies
    E. the material obtained from the interview can usually be obtained at lower cost from existing records

9.____

10. It is desirable and advantageous to leave a maximum measure of planning responsibility to operating agencies or units, rather than to remove the responsibility to a central planning staff agency.
Adoption of the former policy (decentralized planning) would lead to
    A. *less effective* planning; operating personnel do not have the time to make long-term plans
    B. *more effective* planning; operating units are usually better equipped technically than any staff agency and consequently are in a better position to set up valid plans
    C. *less effective* planning; a central planning agency has a more objective point of view than any operating agency can achieve
    D. *more effective* planning; plans are conceived in terms of the existing situation and their execution is carried out with the will to succeed

10.____

4 (2)

E. *less effective* planning; there is little or no opportunity to check deviation from plans in the proposed set-up

Questions 11-15.

DIRECTIONS: The following sections appeared in a report on the work production of two bureaus of a department. Questions 10 through 12 are to be answered on the basis of the following information. Throughout the report, assume that each month has 4 weeks.

Each of the two bureaus maintains a chronological file. In Bureau A, every 9 months on the average, this material fills a standard legal size file cabinet sufficient for 12,000 work units. In Bureau B, the same type of cabinet is filled in 18 months. Each bureau maintains three complete years of information plus a current file. When the current file cabinet is filled, the cabinet containing the oldest material is emptied, the contents disposed of and the cabinet used for current material. The similarity of these operations makes it possible to consolidate these files with little effort.

Study of the practice of using typists as filing clerks for periods when there is no typing work showed (1) Bureau A has for the past 6 months completed a total of 1,500 filing work units a week using on the average 200 man-hours of trained file clerk time and 20 man-hours of typist time, (2) Bureau B has in the same period completed a total of 2,000 filing work units a week using on the average 125 man-hours of trained file clerk time and 60 hours of typist time. This includes all work in chronological files. Assuming that all clerks work at the same speed and that all typists work at the same speed, this indicates that work other than filing should be found for typists or that they should be given some training in the filing procedures used. It should be noted that Bureau A has not been producing the 1,600 units of technical (not filing) work per 30 day period required by Schedule K, but is at present 200 units behind. The Bureau should be allowed 3 working days to get on schedule.

11. What percentage (approximate) of the total number of filing work units completed in both units consists of the work involved in the maintenance of the chronological files?
    A. 5%   B. 10%   C. 15%   D. 20%   E. 25%

11.____

12. If the two chronological files are consolidated, the number of months which should be allowed for filling a cabinet is
    A. 2   B. 4   C. 6   D. 8   E. 14

12.____

13. The MAXIMUM number of file cabinets which can be released for other uses as a result of the consolidation recommended is
    A. 0
    B. 1
    C. 2
    D. 3
    E. not determinable on the basis of the data given

13.____

5 (#2)

14. If all the filing work for both units is consolidated without any diminution in the amount to be done and all filing work is done by trained file clerks, the number of clerks required (35-hour work week) is
    A. 4   B. 5   C. 6   D. 7   E. 8

    14.____

15. In order to comply with the recommendation with respect to Schedule K, the present work production of Bureau A must be increased by
    A. 50%
    B. 100%
    C. 150%
    D. 200%
    E. an amount which is not determinable on the basis of the data given

    15.____

16. A certain training program during World War II resulted in training of thousands of supervisors in industry. The methods of this program were later successfully applied in various governmental agencies. The program was based upon the assumption that there is an irreducible minimum of three supervisory skills. The one of these skills among the following is
    A. to know how to perform the job at hand well
    B. to be able to deal personally with workers, especially face-to-face
    C. to be able to imbue workers with the will to perform the job well
    D. to know the kind of work that is done by one's unit and the policies and procedures of one's agency
    E. the "know-how" of administrative and supervisory processes

    16.____

17. A comment made by an employee about a training course was, *We never have any idea how we are getting along in that course."*
    The fundamental error in training methods to which this criticism points is
    A. insufficient student participation
    B. failure to develop a feeling of need or active want for the material being presented
    C. the training sessions may be too long
    D. no attempt may have been made to connect the new material with what was already known
    E. no goals have been set for the students

    17.____

18. Assume that you are attending a departmental conference on efficiency ratings at which it is proposed that a man-to-man rating scale be introduced.
    You should point out that, of the following, the CHIEF weakness of the man-to-man rating scale is that
    A. it involves abstract numbers rather than concrete employee characteristics
    B. judges are unable to select their own standards for comparison
    C. the standard for comparison shifts from man to man for each person rated
    D. not every person rated is given the opportunity to serve as a standard for comparison
    E. standards for comparison will vary from judge to judge

    18.____

19. Assume that you are conferring with a supervisor who has assigned to his subordinates efficiency ratings which you believe to be generally too low. The supervisor argues that his ratings are generally low because his subordinates are generally inferior.
Of the following, the evidence MOST relevant to the point at issue can be secured by comparing efficiency ratings assigned by this supervisor
    A. with ratings assigned by other supervisors in the same agency
    B. this year with ratings assigned by him in previous years
    C. to men recently transferred to his unit with ratings previously earned by these men
    D. with the general city average of ratings assigned by all supervisors to all employees
    E. with the relative order of merit of his employees as determined independently by promotion test marks

19.____

20. The one of the following which is NOT among the most common of the compensable factors used in wage evaluation studies is
    A. initiative and ingenuity required
    B. physical demand
    C. responsibility for the safety of others
    D. working conditions
    E. presence of avoidable hazards

20.____

21. If independent functions are separated, there is an immediate gain in conserving special skills. If we are to make optimum use of the abilities of our employees, these skills must be conserved.
Assuming the correctness of this statement, it follows that
    A. if we are not making optimum use of employee abilities, independent functions have not been separated
    B. we are making optimum use of employee abilities if we conserve special skills
    C. we are making optimum use of employee abilities if independent functions have been separated
    D. we are not making optimum use of employee abilities if we do not conserve special skills
    E. if special skills are being conserved, independent functions need not be separated

21.____

22. A reorganization of the bureau to provide for a stenographic pool instead of individual unit stenographer will result in more stenographic help being available too each unit when it is required, and consequently will result in greater productivity for each unit. An analysis of the space requirements shows that setting up a stenographic pool will require a minimum of 400 square feet of good space. In order to obtain this space, it will be necessary to reduce the space available for technical personnel, resulting in lesser productivity for each unit.
On the basis of the above discussion, it can be stated that in order to obtain greater productivity for each unit,

22.____

7 (#2)

    A. a stenographic pool should be set up
    B. further analysis of the space requirement should be made
    C. it is not certain as to whether or not a stenographic pool should be set up
    D. the space available for each technician should be increased in order to compensate for the absence of a stenographic pool
    E. a stenographic pool should not be set up

23. The adoption of a single consolidated form will mean that most of the form will not be used in any one operation. This would create waste and confusion. This conclusion is based upon the unstated hypothesis that   23.____
    A. if waste and confusion are to be avoided, a single consolidated form should be used
    B. if a single consolidated form is constructed, most of it can be used in each operation
    C. if waste and confusion are to be avoided, most of the form employed should be used
    D. most of a single consolidated form is not used
    E. a single consolidated form should not be used

24. Assume that you are studying the results of mechanizing several hand operations.   24.____
The type of data which would be MOST useful in proving that an increase in mechanization is followed by a lower cost of operation is data which show that in
    A. some cases a lower cost of operation was not preceded by an increase in mechanization
    B. no case was a higher cost of operation preceded by a decrease in mechanization
    C. some cases a lower cost of operation was preceded by a decrease in mechanization
    D no case was a higher cost of operation preceded by an increase in mechanization
    E. some cases an increase in mechanization was followed by a decrease in cost of operation

25. The type of data which would be MOST useful in determining if an increase in the length of rest periods is followed by an increased rate of production is data which would indicate that _____ in the length of the rest period.   25.____

    A. *decrease* in the total production never follows an increase in
    B. *increase* in the total production never follows an increase
    C. *increase* in the rate of production never follows a decrease
    D. *decrease* in the total production may follow a decrease
    E. *increase* in the total production sometimes follows an increase

KEY (CORRECT ANSWERS)

1.	E		11.	C
2.	B		12.	C
3.	C		13.	B
4.	B		14.	D
5.	E		15.	E
6.	A		16.	B
7.	B		17.	E
8.	A		18.	E
9.	A		19.	C
10.	D		20.	E

21. D
22. C
23. C
24. D
25. A

TEST 3

DIRECTIONS: Each question or incomplete statement is followed by several suggested answers or completions. Select the one that BEST answers the question or completes the statement. *PRINT THE LETTER OF THE CORRECT ANSWER IN THE SPACE AT THE RIGHT.*

1. You have been asked to answer a request from a citizen of the city. After giving the request careful consideration, you find that it cannot be granted. In answering the letter, you should begin by
    A. saying that the request cannot be granted
    B. discussing in detail the consideration you have to the request
    C. quoting the laws relating to the request
    D. explaining in detail why the request cannot be granted
    E. indicating an alternative method of achieving the end desired

    1.____

2. Reports submitted to the department head should be complete to the last detail. A far as possible, summaries should be avoided.
    This statement is, in general,
    A. *correct*; only on the basis of complete information can a proper decision be reached
    B. *incorrect*; if all reports submitted were of this character, a department head would never complete his work
    C. *correct*; the decision as to what is important and what is not can only be made by the person who is responsible for the action
    D. *incorrect*; preliminary reports, obviously, cannot be complete to the last detail
    E. *correct*; summaries tend to conceal the actual state of affairs and to encourage generalizations which would not be made if the details were known; consequently, they should be avoided if possible

    2.____

3. The supervisor of a large bureau, who was required in the course of business to answer a large number of letters from the public, completely formalized his responses, that is, the form and vocabulary of every letter he prepared were the same as far as possible.
    This method of solving the problem of how to handle correspondence is, in general
    A. *good*; it reduces the time and thought necessary for a response
    B. *bad*; the time required to develop a satisfactory standard form and vocabulary is usually not available in an active organization
    C. *good*; the use of standard forms causes similar requests to be answered in a similar way
    D. *bad*; the use of standard forms and vocabulary to the extent indicated results in letters in *officialese* hindering unambiguous explanation and clear understanding
    E. *good*; if this method were applied to an entire department, the answering of letters could be left to clerks and the administrators would be free for more constructive work

    3.____

4. Of the following systems of designating the pages in a looseleaf manual subject to constant revision and addition, the MOST practicable one is to use _____ for main divisions and _____ for subdivisions.
   A. decimals; integers
   B. integers; letters
   C. integers; decimals
   D. letters; integers
   E. integers; integers

5. A subordinate submits a proposed draft of a form which is being revised to facilitate filling in the form on a typewriter. The draft shows that the captions for each space will be printed below the space to be filled in.
   This proposal is
   A. *undesirable*; it decreases visibility
   B. *desirable*; it makes the form easy to understand
   C. *undesirable*; it makes the form more difficult to understand
   D. *desirable*; it increases visibility
   E. *undesirable*; it is less compact than other layouts

6. The one of the following which is NOT an essential element of an integrated reporting system for work-measurement is a
   A. uniform record form for accumulating data and instructions for its maintenance
   B. procedure for routing reports upward through the organization and routing summaries downward
   C. standard report form for summarizing basic records and instructions for its preparation
   D. method for summarizing, analyzing and presenting data from several reports
   E. looseleaf revisable manual which contains all procedural materials that are reasonably permanent and have a substantial reference value

7. Forms control only accomplishes the elimination, consolidation, and simplification of forms. It contributes little to the elimination, consolidation, and simplification of procedures.
   This statement is
   A. *correct*; the form is static while the procedure is dynamic; consequently, control of one does not necessarily result in control of the other
   B. *incorrect*; forms frequently dictate the way work is laid out; consequently, control of one frequently results in control of the other
   C. *correct*; the procedure is primary and the form secondary; consequently, control of procedure will also control form
   D. *incorrect*; the form and procedure are identical from the viewpoint of work control; consequently, control of one means control of the other
   E. *correct*; the assurance that forms are produced and distributed economically has little relationship to the consolidation and simplification of procedures

8. Governmental agencies frequently attempt to avoid special interest group pressures by referring them to the predetermined legislative policy, or to the necessity for rules and regulations applying generally to all groups and situations.
Of the following, the MOST important weakness of this formally correct position is that
   A. it is not tenable in the face of determined opposition
   B. it tends to legalize and formalize the informal relationships between citizen groups and the government
   C. the achievement of an agency's aims is in large measure dependent upon its ability to secure the cooperation and support of special interest groups
   D. independent groups which participate in the formulation of policy in their sphere of interest tend to criticize openly and to press for changes in the direction of their policy
   E. agencies following this policy find it difficult to decentralize their public relation activities as subdivisions can only refer to the agency's overall policy

8.____

9. One of the primary purposes of the performance budget is to improve the ability to examine budgetary requirement by groups who have not been engaged in the construction of the budget.
This is accomplished by
   A. making line by line appropriations
   B. making lump sum appropriations by department
   C. enumerating authorization for all expenditures
   D. standardizing the language used and the kinds of authorizations permitted
   E. permitting examination on the level of accomplishment

9.____

10. When engaged in budget construction or budget analysis, there is no point in trying to determine the total or average benefits to be obtained from total expenditures for a particular commodity or function.
The validity of this argument is USUALLY based upon the
   A. viewpoint that it is not possible to construct a functional budget
   B. theory (or phenomenon) of diminishing utility
   C. hypothesis that as governmental budgets provide in theory for minimum requirements, there is no need to determine total benefits
   D. assumption that such determinations are not possible
   E. false hypothesis that a comparison between expected and achieved results does not aid in budget construction

10.____

Questions 11-12.

DIRECTIONS: Questions 11 and 12 are to be answered on the basis of the following paragraph.

   Production planning is mainly a process of synthesis. As a basis for the positive act of bringing complex production elements properly together, however, analysis is necessary, especially if improvement is to be made in an existing organization. The necessary analysis requires customary means of orientation and preliminary fact gathering with emphasis, however, on the recognition of administrative goals and of the relationship among work steps.

11. The entire process described is PRIMARILY one of 11.____
    A. taking apart, examining, and recombining
    B. deciding what changes are necessary, making the changes and checking on their value
    C. fact finding so as to provide the necessary orientation
    D. discovering just where the emphasis in production should be placed and then modifying the existing procedure so that it is placed properly
    E. recognizing administrative goals and the relationship among work steps

12. In production planning according to the above paragraph, analysis is used PRIMARILY as 12.____
    A. a means of making important changes in an organization
    B. the customary means of orientation and preliminary fact finding
    C. a development of the relationship among work steps
    D. a means for holding the entire process intact by providing a logical basis
    E. a method to obtain the facts upon which a theory can be built

Questions 13-15.

DIRECTIONS: Questions 13 through 15 are to be answered on the basis of the following paragraph.

Public administration is policy-making. But it is not autonomous, exclusive or isolated policy-making. It is policy-making on a field where mighty forces contend, forces engendered in and by society. It is policy-making subject to still other and various policy makers. Public administration is one of a number of basic political processes by which these people achieves and controls government.

13. From the point of view expressed in the above paragraph, public administration is 13.____
    A. becoming a technical field with completely objective processes
    B. the primary force in modern society
    C. a technical field which should be divorced from the actual decision-making function
    D. basically anti-democratic
    E. intimately related to politics

14. According to the above paragraph, public administration is NOT entirely 14.____
    A. a force generated in and by society
    B. subject at times to controlling influences
    C. a social process
    D. policy-making relating to administrative practices
    E. related to policy-making at lower levels

15. The above paragraph asserts that public administration 15.____
    A. develops the basic and controlling policies
    B. is the result of policies made by many different forces
    C. should attempt to break through its isolated policy-making and engage on a broader field
    D. is a means of directing government
    E. is subject to the political processes by which acts are controlled

Questions 16-18.

DIRECTIONS: Questions 16 through 18 are to be answered on the basis of the following chart.

In order to understand completely the source of an employee's insecurity on his job, it is necessary to understand how he came to be, who he is and what kind of person he is away from his job. This would necessitate an understanding of those personal assets and liabilities which the employee brings to the job situation. These arise from his individual characteristics and his past experiences and established patterns of interpersonal relations. This whole area is of tremendous scope, encompassing everything included within the study of psychiatry and interpersonal relations. Therefore, it has been impracticable to consider it in detail. Attention has been focused on the relatively circumscribed area of the actual occupational situation. The factors considered those which the employee brings to the job situation and which arise from his individual characteristics and his past experience and established patterns of interpersonal relations are: intellectual-level or capacity, specific aptitudes, education, work experience, health, social and economic background, patterns of interpersonal relations and resultant personality characteristics.

16. According to the above paragraph, the one of the following fields of study which would be of LEAST importance in the study of the problem is the 16.____
    A. relationships existing among employees
    B. causes of employee insecurity in the job situation
    C. conflict, if it exists, between intellectual level and work experience
    D. distribution of intellectual achievement
    E. relationship between employee characteristics and the established pattern of interpersonal relations in the work situation

17. According to the above paragraph, in order to make a thoroughgoing and comprehensive study of the sources of employee insecurity, the field of study should include 17.____
    A. only such circumscribed areas as are involved in extra-occupational situations
    B. a study of the dominant mores of the period
    C. all branches of the science of psychology
    D. a determination of the characteristics, such as intellectual capacity, which an employee should bring to the job situation
    E. employee personality characteristics arising from previous relationships with other people

18. It is implied by this paragraph that it would be of GREATEST advantage to bring 18._____
to this problem a comprehensive knowledge of
   A. all established patterns of interpersonal relations
   B. the milieu in which the employee group is located
   C. what assets and liabilities are presented in the job situation
   D. methods of focusing attention on relatively circumscribed regions
   E. the sources of an employee's insecurity on his job

Questions 19-20.

DIRECTIONS: Questions 19 and 20 are to be answered on the basis of the following paragraph.

If, during a study, some hundreds of values of a variable (such as annual number of latenesses for each employee in a department) have been noted merely in the arbitrary order in which they happen to occur, the mind cannot properly grasp the significance of the record, the observations must be ranked or classified in some way before the characteristics of the series can be comprehended, and those comparisons, on which arguments as to causation depend, can be made with other series. A dichotomous classification is too crude; if the values are merely classified according to whether they exceed or fall short of some fixed value, a large part of the information given by the original record is lost. Numerical measurements lend themselves with peculiar readiness to a manifold classification.

19. According to the above paragraph, if the values of a variable which are gathered 19._____
during a study are classified in a few subdivisions, the MOST likely result will be
   A. an inability to grasp the signification of the record
   B. an inability to relate the series with other series
   C. a loss of much of the information in the original data
   D. a loss of the readiness with which numerical measurements lend themselves to a manifold classification
   E. that the order in which they happen to occur will be arbitrary

20. The above paragraph advocates, with respect to numerical data, the use of 20._____
   A. arbitrary order   B. comparisons with other series
   C. a two-value classification   D. a many value classification
   E. all values of a variable

Questions 21-25.

DIRECTIONS: Questions 21 through 25 are to be answered on the basis of the following chart.

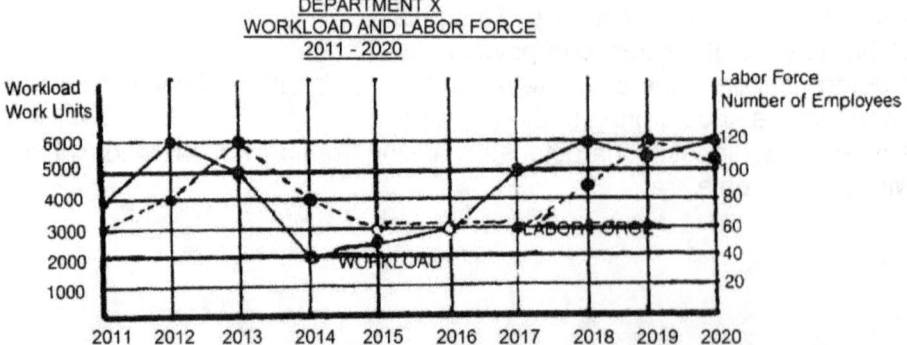

7 (#3)

21. The one of the following years for which average employee production was 21.____
LOWEST was
A. 2012   B. 2014   C. 2016   D. 2018   E. 2020

22. The average annual employee production for the ten-year period was, in 22.____
terms of work units, MOST NEARLY
A. 30   B. 50   C. 70   D. 80   E. 90

23. On the basis of the chart, it can be deduced that personnel needs for the 23.____
coming year are budgeted on the basis of
A. workload for the current year
B. expected workload for the coming year
C. no set plan
D. average workload over the five years immediately preceding the period
E. expected workload for the five coming years

24. The chart indicates that the operation is carefully programmed and that the labor 24.____
force has been used properly.
This opinion is
A. *supported* by the chart; the organization has been able to meet emergency situations requiring much additional work without commensurate increase in staff
B. *not supported* by the chart; the irregular workload shows a complete absence of planning
C. *supported* by the chart; the similar shapes of the workload and labor force curves show that these important factors are closely related
D. *not supported* by the chart; poor planning with respect to labor requirements is obvious from the chart
E. *supported* by the chart; the average number of units of work performed in any 5-year period during the 10 years shows sufficient regularity to indicate a definite trend

25. The chart indicates that the department may be organized in such a way as to 25.____
require a permanent minimum staff which is too large for the type of operation indicated.
This opinion is
A. *supported* by the chart; there is indication that the operation calls for an irreducible minimum number of employees and application of the most favorable work production records shows this to be too high for normal operation
B. *not supported* by the chart; the absence of any sort of regularity makes it impossible to express any opinion with any degree of certainty
C. *supported* by the chart; the expected close relationship between workload and labor force is displaced somewhat, a phenomenon which usually occurs as a result of a fixed minimum requirement
D. *not supported* by the chart; the violent movement of the labor force curve makes it evident that no minimum requirements are in effect

E. *supported* by the chart; calculation shows that the average number of employees was 84 with an average variation of 17.8, thus indicating that the minimum number of 60 persons was too high for efficient operation

---

KEY (CORRECT ANSWERS)

1.	A	11.	A
2.	B	12.	E
3.	D	13.	E
4.	C	14.	D
5.	A	15.	D
6.	E	16.	D
7.	B	17.	E
8.	C	18.	B
9.	E	19.	C
10.	B	20.	D

21. B
22. B
23. A
24. D
25. A

EXAMINATION SECTION

TEST 1

DIRECTIONS: Each question or incomplete statement is followed by several suggested answers or completions. Select the one that BEST answers the question or completes the statement. *PRINT THE LETTER OF THE CORRECT ANSWER IN THE SPACE AT THE RIGHT.*

1. The new head of a central filing unit, after studying a procedure in use, decided that it was unsatisfactory. He thereupon drew up an entirely new procedure which made no use of and ignored the existing procedure.
   This plan of action is, in general,
   A. *satisfactory*; a new broom sweeps clean
   B. *unsatisfactory*; any plan should use available resources to the utmost before resorting to new creation
   C. *satisfactory*; in general, use of part of an old procedure and part of a new procedure results sin an unworkable patchwork arrangement
   D. *unsatisfactory*; before deciding that the existing procedure was unusable, he should have requested that an independent, unbiased agency study the problem
   E. *satisfactory*; it is usually less time consuming to construct a new plan than to remedy an old one

1.____

2. Assume that you have broken a complex job into simpler and smaller components.
   After you have assigned a component to each employee, should you proceed to teach each employee a number of alternative methods for doing his job?
   A. *yes*; the more methods for performing a job an employee knows, the more chance there is that he will choose the one best suited to his abilities
   B. *No*; experienced employees should be permitted to decide how to perform the jobs assigned to them
   C. *Yes*; if several different methods are available, a desirable flexibility of operation results
   D. *No*; a single method for each job should be decided upon and taught
   E. *Yes*; the employees will have greater interest in their jobs

2.____

3. Assume that you are the head of a major staff unit and that a line unit has requested from your unit a special report to be completed in one day. After reviewing the request, you decide that much tie would be saved if two items which you know are superfluous are omitted from the report. You discuss the matter with the head of the other unit and he still insists that the two items are essential for his purposes.
   The one of the following actions which you should take at this stage is to
   A. plan to complete the report, including the two items, as expeditiously as possible
   B. write a memorandum to the department head giving both opinions fairly and asking for a decision

3.____

2 (#1)

C. plan to complete the report without the two items, as expeditiously as possible
D. devise a plan for preparing the report without the two items which will permit you to add them later if they prove necessary although some time may be lost
E. again review the report with the line unit showing them why the two items are unnecessary

4. The one of the following functions of a supervisor which can be MOST success- 4.____
fully delegated is
   A. responsibility for accomplishing the unit's mission
   B. handling discipline
   C. checking completed work
   D. reporting to the bureau chief
   E. placing subordinates in the proper job

5. It is a standard operating procedure in an office which receives several 5.____
thousand forms each week to have the file on clerk accumulate a week's receipts before filing them. The forms will not be examined for a period of one month after receipt.
In comparison with daily filing, this procedure is, in general,
   A. *less satisfactory*; it keeps the files unnecessarily incomplete
   B. *more satisfactory*; it tends to reduce filing time
   C. *less satisfactory*; all information should be placed in a safe storage place as soon as possible
   D. *more satisfactory*; it tends to eliminate the prefiling period
   E. *less satisfactory*; it tends to build up an unnecessary period

6. Some organizations attempt to keep a constant backlog of work. 6.____
This procedure is usually
   A. *undesirable*; reports are not ready when they are needed
   B. *desirable*; it tends to insure continuity of work flow
   C. *undesirable*; production records are too difficult to keep
   D. *desirable*; it tends to keep the employees under constant pressure
   E. *undesirable*; it tends to keep the employees under constant pressure

7. The first few times a procedure is carried through, a close check should be kept 7.____
of all work times.
The PRIMARY reason for this is to
   A. be able to present a clear picture of the situation
   B. determine if the employees understand the procedure
   C. evaluate the efficiency which may have been presented by the new procedure
   D. determine the efficiency of the employees
   E. permit revision of schedules

8. The one of the following pieces of information which is of LEAST importance in setting up the schedule for a given job is the time 8._____
   A. which is required to perform each component of the job
   B. when the source material will be available
   C. the job will take under adverse conditions
   D. by which the job must be completed
   E. employees will be available

9. Every employee should have a thorough knowledge of the organization of which he is a part. 9._____
   Of the following, the BEST justification for the above opinion is that
   A. the feeling of being a member of a team develops a responsible attitude toward one's everyday duties
   B. in an emergency, an employee may be called upon to perform duties other than his own
   C. the intricate details of an organization as complicated as a city department cannot easily be reduced to an organization chart
   D. an understanding of the different specialized units in an organization is often necessary to achieve the organization's given objective
   E. many city jobs are technical; thus, each employee should be trained to have more than a single narrow skill

10. The one of the following which is NOT a good rule in administering discipline is for you as a supervisor to 10._____
    A. reprimand the employee in private even though the fault was committed before others
    B. allow the employee a chance to reply to your criticism if he wishes
    C. be as specific as possible in criticizing the employee for his faults
    D. be sure you have all the facts before you reprimand an employee for an error he has committed
    E. allow an extended period to elapse after an error has been committed before reprimanding an employee

11. After you have submitted your annual evaluations of the work of your subordinates, one of them whose work has not been satisfactory complains to you that your evaluation was unjustified. 11._____
    For you to avoid discussing the evaluation but to point out two or three specific instances where the employee's work was below standard is
    A. *desirable*; an employee should be told what aspects of his work are unsatisfactory
    B. *undesirable*; once the evaluation has been submitted, there is no point in reconsidering it
    C. *desirable*; once the evaluation has been submitted, there is no point in reconsidering it but a discussion of the employee's weaknesses may help
    D. *undesirable*; it would have been better to explain how you arrived at your evaluation
    E. *desirable*; entering into a general argument is bad for the discipline of an organization

12. The chief of a central files bureau which has 50 employees customarily spends   12.____
a considerable portion of his time in spot-checking the files, reviewing material
being transferred from active to inactive files and similar activities.
From the viewpoint of the department top management, the MOST pertinent
evaluation which can be made on the basis of this information is that the
   A. supervisor is conscientious and hardworking
   B. bureau may need additional staff
   C. supervisor has not made a sufficient delegation of authority and
      responsibility
   D. bureau needs an in-service training course as the work of its employees
      requires an abnormal amount of review
   E. filing system employed may be inadequate

13. Assume that you are in charge of a unit with 40 employees. The department   13.____
head requests immediate preparation of a special and rather complicated
report which will take about a day to complete if everyone in your unit works on
it.
After breaking the job into simple components and assigning each component
to an employee, should more than one person be instructed on the procedure
to be followed on each component?
   A. *No*; the procedure would be a waste of time in this instance
   B. *Yes*; it is always desirable to have a replacement available in the event of
      illness or any other emergency
   C. *No*; in general, as long as an employee's job performance is satisfactory,
      there is no need to train an alternate
   D. *Yes*; the presence of more than one person in a unit who can perform a
      given task tends to prevent the formation of a bottleneck
   E. *No*; there is, in general, no need to train more than one employee in the
      performance of a special job

14. A new employee who has shown that she is capable of performing superior work   14.____
during the first month of her employment falls far below this standard after the
first month.
For the supervisor to wait until the end of the probationary period and then
recommend that she be discharged if her work is still unsatisfactory is
   A. *undesirable*; she should have been discharged when her work became
      unsatisfactory
   B. *desirable*; there is no place in the civil service for unsatisfactory
      employees
   C. *undesirable*; he should immediately attempt to determine the cause of the
      poor performance
   D. *desirable*; the employee is entitled to an opportunity to prove herself
   E. *undesirable*; the employee is obviously capable of performing good work
      and simply requires some guidance from the supervisor

15. In order to make sure that work is completed on time, the unit supervisor should   15.____
    A. use the linear method of delegating responsibility
    B. pitch in and do as much of the work himself as he can
    C. schedule the work and keep himself informed of its progress
    D. not assign more than one person to any one task
    E. know the capabilities of his subordinates

16. One of the more effective ways to obtain optimum performance from employees   16.____
    is to keep them off balance by not letting them feel secure in the job; to permit
    an employee to feel secure is to invite him to settle into a comfortable rut.
    The point of view expressed in this statement is
    A. *correct*; studies have shown that the degree of effort put forth on a job
       generally varies directly with the degree of job insecurity
    B. *incorrect*; studies have shown that a relatively high degree of security is
       conducive to best job performance
    C. *correct*; while studies have shown that there is little relationship between
       security and job performance, what tendencies are present to support the
       point of view expressed
    D. *incorrect*; studies have shown that there is little relationship between
       security and job performance and what tendencies are present are
       opposed to the point of view expressed
    E. *correct*; while no specific studies have been made in this field, analogous
       studies made in similar fields show that permitting a feeling of security to
       develop results in decreased job performance

Questions 17-19.

DIRECTIONS: Questions 17 through 19 are to be answered on the basis of the following
paragraph.

The supervisor of a large clerical and statistical division has assigned to one of the units
under his supervision the preparation of a special statistical report required by the department
head. The unit accepted the assignment without comment but soon ran into considerable
difficulty because no one in his unit had had any statistical training.

17. If a result of this lack of training is that the report is not completed on time,   17.____
    although everyone has done all that could be expected, the responsibility for
    the failure rests with
    A. the department head   B. the supervisor
    C. the unit head   D. the employees in the unit
    E. no one

18. This incident indicates that the supervisory staff has insufficient knowledge of   18.____
    employee
    A. capabilities
    B. reaction to increased demands
    C. on-the-job training needs
    D. work habits
    E. ability to perform ordinary assignments

19. After working on the report for two days, the unit head notifies the supervisor that he will not be able to get the report out in the required time. He states that his staff will be completely trained in another day or two and that after preparing the report will be a simple matter. At this stage, the supervisor decides to have the statistical unit prepare the report.
    This action on the part of the supervisor is
    A. *undesirable*; the unit head should be given an incentive to continue with his training program which may produce good results
    B. *desirable*; it is the most effective way in which the supervisor can show his displeasure with the unit head's failure
    C. *undesirable*; it may adversely affect the morale of the unit
    D. *desirable*; it will generally result in a better report completed in a shorter time
    E. *undesirable*; the time spent training the unit will be completely wasted

20. A supervisor criticizes a subordinate's work by telling him that he is disappointed with it. The supervisor states that the work is completely unsatisfactory, shows where it is bad, and says that improvement is expected.
    This approach is usually
    A. *good*; the employee knows just where he stands
    B. *poor*; some favorable comment should be made at the same time if possible
    C. *good*; it is good policy to keep this type of interview as short as possible
    D. *poor*; the employee should be asked to explain why his work is poor
    E. *good*; the supervisor did not criticize the subordinate in front of other employees

Questions 21-25.

DIRECTIONS: Column I below lists five kinds of statistical data which are to be transformed into a chart or a graph for incorporation into the department annual report. Column II lists nine different kinds of graphs or charts. For each type of information listed in Column I, select the chart or graph from Column II by means of which it should be demonstrated.

COLUMN I

21. The relationship between employees' occupational classification and their salaries, for all employees by occupational classification, showing minimum, maximum, and average salary in each group.

22. A comparison of the number of employees in the department, the departmental budget the number of employees in the operating divisions and the operating division budget for each year over a ten-year period.

COLUMN I	COLUMN II
23. The amount of money spent for each of the department's 10 most important functions during the past year.	D.  23.____
24. The percentage of the department's budget spent for each of the department's activities for each year over a ten-year period.	E.  24.____
25. The number of each kind of employee employed in the department over a period of twenty years and the total number of employees in the department for each of these periods.	F. 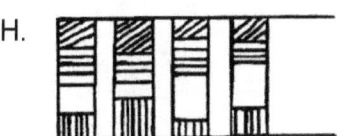 25.____
	G. 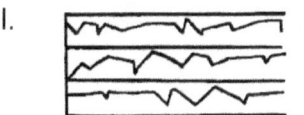
	H.
	I.

KEY (CORRECT ANSWERS)

1.	B		11.	D
2.	D		12.	C
3.	A		13.	A
4.	C		14.	C
5.	B		15.	C
6.	B		16.	B
7.	E		17.	B
8.	C		18.	A
9.	A		19.	D
10.	E		20.	B

21. F
22. D
23. C
24. H
25. G

TEST 2

DIRECTIONS: Each question or incomplete statement is followed by several suggested answers or completions. Select the one that BEST answers the question or completes the statement. *PRINT THE LETTER OF THE CORRECT ANSWER IN THE SPACE AT THE RIGHT.*

1. The report of the head of Unit Y to his bureau chief on the performance of a new clerical employee indicates that the performance is not up to the expected standard. After reading the report, the bureau chief transferred the employee to Unit X.
   This action on the part of the bureau chief was
   A. in line with good personal practice; an employee who does poorly in one place may do better in another
   B. premature; an attempt to discover the cause of the poor performance should be made first
   C. desirable; personnel reports become meaningless unless acted upon at once
   D. undesirable; unsatisfactory employees should be dismissed and not transferred from unit to unit
   E. in the best interest of the organization; whenever a supervisor cannot get along with a subordinate for whatever reason, it is desirable to transfer the subordinate

   1.____

2. Suppose that you have been consulted by a department head who wishes to initiate an in-service training course in his department. The department head suggests that, as a first step, a training course be initiated for supervisors in the department.
   This suggestion is BEST characterized as
   A. *undesirable*; the supervisors are generally the persons least in need of work incentives
   B. *desirable*; it is generally cheaper and more effective to train a few supervisors than a large number of employees
   C. *undesirable*; supervisors may be held up to ridicule if they are isolated for training
   D. *desirable*; trained supervisors are needed to train employees
   E. *undesirable*; employees should be trained before supervisors

   2.____

3. Any person thoroughly familiar with the specific steps in a particular class of work is well qualified to serve as a training course instructor in that work.
   This statement is erroneous CHIEFLY because
   A. it is practically impossible for any instructor to be acquainted with all the specific steps sin a particular class of work
   B. what is true of one class of work is not necessarily true of other types of work
   C. a qualified instructor cannot be expected to have detailed information about many specific fields

   3.____

D. the steps in any type of work are usually interrelated and not independent or unique
E. the quantity of information possessed by an instructor does not bear a direct relationship to the quality of instruction

4. Of the following, the MOST significant argument against making it compulsory for civil service employees to attend a training course is that
    A. unwilling trainees will be penalized in any event by non-promotion
    B. most training requires additional time and expense on the part of the trainee
    C. training is highly desirable but not absolutely essential for adequate job performance
    D. incompetent work is generally reflected in poor service ratings
    E. trainees must be receptive if training is to be successful

5. There are four basic systems of job evaluation which have been extensively used by government and industry.
   The one of the following which is NOT one of these is the _____ system.
    A. Benchmark
    B. Factor Comparison
    C. Point
    D. Job Classification
    E. Ranking

6. Of the following, the CHIEF advantage derived by filling all vacancies in an organization by promotion from below rather than from outside the organization is that such a procedure
    A. fills existing vacancies from the widest possible recruitment base
    B. stimulates individual employees to improve their work habits
    C. avoids personality difficulties likely to arise when an employee is assigned to supervise former colleagues
    D. indirectly coordinates the work of different units by interchange of personnel
    E. encourages reorientation and review of administrative procedures

7. Of the following, the CHIEF justification for a periodic classification audit is that
    A. salaries should be readjusted at frequent intervals
    B. some degree of personnel turnover should always be expected
    C. a career service requires regular promotion opportunities
    D. employees require frequent stimulation and encouragement
    E. positions frequently change over a period of time

8. A classification analyst sorts jobs horizontally and vertically.
   Of the following, the LEAST important job factor to be considered with respect to vertical placement is
    A. independence of action and decision
    B. consequence of errors
    C. kind and character of work performed
    D. degree of supervision received
    E. determination of policy

9. Assume that you have been assigned to prepare a plan for conducting a large scale job classification survey.
   Of the following, the BEST suggestion for reducing the number of appeals from the final allocations likely to be received after the classification study has been completed is to
   A. have supervisors check statements of employees on classification questionnaires
   B. allocate present positions to proposed classes according to jurisdictional assignments
   C. adjust salary to present level of work performed by employees
   D. allow employee participation throughout the classification process
   E. postpone controversial problems until simpler problems have been solved and a general blueprint laid down

10. A comment made by an employee about a training course was, *Oh, I suppose it's important for the job but it's a waste of time for me just to sit in that course and yawn while the instructor rambles on."*
    The fundamental error in training methodology to which this criticism points is failure to provide
    A. goals for the students
    B. for individual differences
    C. connecting links between new and old material
    D. for student participation
    E. motivation for the subject matter of the course

11. You are preparing a long report addressed to your superior on a study which you have conducted for him.
    The one of the following sections which should come FIRST in the report is a
    A. description of the working procedure utilized in the study
    B. description of the situation which exists
    C. summary of the conclusions of the survey
    D. discussion of possible objections to the report and their refutation
    E. description of the method of installing the recommendations

12. While setting up a reporting system to help the department planning section, an administrator proposed the policy that no overlap or duplication be permitted even if it meant that some minor areas were left uncovered.
    This policy is
    A. *undesirable*; overlap is frequently necessary
    B. *desirable*; the presence of overlap and duplication indicates defective planning
    C. *undesirable*; setting up general policy in advance of the specific reporting system may lead to inflexibility
    D. *desirable*; it is not necessary to get complete coverage in order to be able to plan operations
    E. *undesirable*; duplication is preferable to leaving any area uncovered

Questions 13-15.

DIRECTIONS: Questions 13 through 15 are to be answered on the basis of the following paragraph.

Prior to revising its child care program, a department feels that it is necessary to get some information from the mothers served by the existing program in order to determine where changes are required. A questionnaire is to be constructed to obtain this information.

13. Of the following points which can be taken into consideration in the construction of the questionnaire, the one which is of LEAST importance is
    A. that the data are to be put into punch cards
    B. the aspects of the program which seem to be in need of change
    C. the type of person who will fill out the questionnaire
    D. testing the questionnaire for ambiguity in advance of general distribution
    E. setting up a control group so that answers received can be compared to a standard

13.____

14. To discuss this questionnaire with all mothers who have been asked to answer it, before they actually fill it out, is
    A. *desirable*; the mothers may be able to offer valuable suggestions for changes in the form of the questionnaire
    B. *undesirable*; it is of some value but consumes too much valuable time
    C. *desirable*; cooperation and uniform interpretation will tend to be achieved
    D. *undesirable*; it may cause the answers to be biased
    E. *desirable*; the group will tend to support the program

14.____

15. Of the following items included in the questionnaire, the one which will be of LEAST assistance for comparing attitudes toward the program among different kinds of persons is
    A. name
    B. address
    C. age
    D. place of birth
    E. education

15.____

16. You have been asked, to prepare for public distribution, a statement dealing with a controversial matter.
    Of the following approaches, the one which would usually be MOST effective is to present your department's point of view
    A. as tersely as possible with no reference to any other matters
    B. developed from ideas and facts well known to most readers
    C. and show all the statistical data and techniques which were used in arriving at it
    D. in such a way that the controversial parts are omitted
    E. substantiated by supporting quotations from persons in the specialized field even if they are not well known

16.____

5 (#2)

17. During a conference of administrative staff personnel, the department head discussing the letter prepared for his signature stated, *"Use no more words than are necessary to express your meaning."*
Following this rule in letter writing is, in general,
    A. *desirable*; considerable time will be saved in the preparation of correspondence
    B. *undesirable*; it is frequently necessary to elaborate on an explanation in order to make certain that the reader will understand
    C. *desirable*; terse statements give government letters a business-like air which impresses readers favorably
    D. *undesirable*; terse statements are generally cold and formal and produce an unfavorable reaction in the reader
    E. *desirable*; the use of more words than are necessary is likely to obscure the meaning and tire the reader

17.____

18. While you are designing the layout for a departmental procedure manual, it is suggested that you carefully arrange your reading material so that there will be a minimum amount of blank space on the page.
Of the following judgments of this suggestion, the one which is the MOST valid basis for action is that it is
    A. *bad*; readability and ease of reference will be decreased
    B. *good*; the cost of production can be decreased considerably without any great disadvantage
    C. *of little or no importance*; more or less blank space on the page will not affect the value of the manual
    D. *good*; it will make for a smaller, easier to handle book
    E. *bad*; replacement of outdated pages is made more difficult by having more material on a page

18.____

19. After the planning of an employee's procedure manual had been completed, the suggestion was made that the manual should be prepared and arranged so that changes could be made readily.
Of the following decisions with respect to this suggestion, the one which is MOST desirable from the viewpoint of good administration is that the suggestions should
    A. not be considered as it is generally impossible to prepare a satisfactory manual which will take everything into consideration
    B. be followed only if it does not conflict with the planned layout
    C. be used even if it is somewhat more costly than the planned layout
    D. be noted and acted upon at the next revision of the manual
    E. not be considered as this type of manual is more difficult to maintain properly

19.____

20. Assume that you are in charge of preparing a procedure manual of about 100 pages for a large clerical unit. After you have decided to use a looseleaf format, one of your subordinates proposes that only one side of the page be printed.

20.____

This proposal is
- A. *good*; replacement of obsolete pages is made easier
- B. *poor*; cost is increased
- C. *good*; provision is automatically made for employee's notes
- D. *poor*; it will increase the size of the manual, making it more difficult to use
- E. *good*; indexing will be made easier

21. It may be assumed that if all departments had qualified personnel officers, not all departments would be lacking adequate training programs. However, the most cursory examination of the situation will show that some departments do not have adequate training programs. Thus, we must conclude that some of them lack qualified personnel officers.
    The argument presented in the report is
    - A. *correct*; the conclusion follows logically from the assumption and the facts
    - B. *not correct*; what can be concluded is that no department has a qualified personnel officer
    - C. *not correct*; no conclusion with respect to the presence of personnel officers in departments can be drawn from the information
    - D. *not correct*; what can be concluded is that the absence of an adequate training program in a department implies the absence of a personnel officer
    - E. *correct*; but the conclusion is false as the hypothesis is not true

22. In a study of the relationship between a fixed discipline policy and the incidence of lateness, it would be MOST informative to have data proving the statement:
    - A. In those organizations in which there are no fixed discipline policy, the incidence of lateness is variable.
    - B. The incidence of lateness has not decreased in those organizations where fixed discipline policies have been abandoned.
    - C. The incidence of lateness and the discipline policy vary from organization to organization.
    - D. Discipline policies sometimes ignore the problem of lateness.
    - E. In organizations with a fixed discipline policy, the incidence of lateness is variable.

23. The data prove that an increase in the number of clerks performing filing work results in an increased cost per item filed.
    On the basis of these data, we can be certain that
    - A. if filing costs per item filed increase, it is caused by an increase in the number of clerks filing
    - B. if filing costs per item filed decrease, the number of clerks filing cannot be increasing
    - C. if the number of clerks filing is changed, the unit cost per filing will change
    - D. if the number of clerks filing is not increased, the cost per unit filed will not increase
    - E. if the number of clerks filing is decreased, the cost per item filed will decrease

24. Each unit either has sufficient space assigned to it or it has not. No unit which has insufficient space assigned to it has neglected to ask for additional space. From these data, we can state
    A. units with sufficient space have not asked for additional space
    B. only units which have sufficient space have not asked for additional space
    C. nothing about the relationship between the need for additional space and requests made for additional space
    D. all units which have requested additional space have insufficient space
    E. no units which have requested additional space have sufficient space

24.____

25. One argument which is presented against a strict career system in the civil service is as follows:
The employees who are recruited today for low-level jobs become the administrators of tomorrow. At the present time the employees we are attracting for the low-level jobs are untrained and poorly educated. Thus, it follows that the administrators of tomorrow will be untrained and poorly educated.
The one of the following which is a CORRECT criticism of the reasoning is that
    A. the argument is logically correct but the conclusion is false as the hypothesis that we are attracting untrained and poorly educated people for our low-level job is false
    B. the conclusion does not follow logically from hypotheses
    C. the argument is logically correct, but the conclusion is false because it is a false hypothesis that tomorrow's administrators will come from employees who hold low-level jobs
    D. the argument is logically correct and the conclusion is correct
    E. while the argument is logically correct and the hypotheses are not demonstrably false, the argument ignores the realities of the case that those who are untrained today may be trained tomorrow

25.____

KEY (CORRECT ANSWERS)

1. B
2. D
3. E
4. E
5. A

6. B
7. E
8. C
9. D
10. D

11. C
12. E
13. E
14. C
15. A

16. B
17. E
18. A
19. C
20. A

21. C
22. B
23. B
24. B
25. B

TEST 3

DIRECTIONS: Each question or incomplete statement is followed by several suggested answers or completions. Select the one that BEST answers the question or completes the statement. *PRINT THE LETTER OF THE CORRECT ANSWER IN THE SPACE AT THE RIGHT.*

1. Surveying modern administration, it becomes clear that there is GREATEST need at present for administrators with   1.____
    A. a good knowledge of personnel administration
    B. the ability to write good reports
    C. a working knowledge of modern methods analysis
    D. a broad rather than specialized viewpoint
    E. the ability to analyze complicated fiscal programs

2. The one of the following which is a fundamental obstacle to effective planning in MOST governmental agencies is   2.____
    A. inadequate staff or resources
    B. the absence of the properly centralized administration
    C. the absence of clearly defined objective and constituent programs
    D. the neglect of analysis of ways and means
    E. the absence of functional boundaries for units and individuals

3. A department consists of several independent bureaus, each responsible to the commissioner for its own planning, operation, and reporting, a central personnel unit and the commissioner's office consisting of a secretary and several clerks to handle public relations.   3.____
   The one of the following *undesirable* characteristics which is MOST likely to arise in this organization is
    A. absence of planning
    B. weak and ineffectual leadership
    C. failure to have employees properly trained
    D. a lack of an easily understandable goal
    E. duplication of work

4. The one of the following practices which is MOST likely to lead to confusion, recrimination and jurisdictional conflict among the bureaus of a department is the failure to   4.____
    A. make clear and unambiguous assignments
    B. systematically subdivide the work
    C. explain general policy to those responsible for its achievement
    D. allocate equitably available resources
    E. set up uniform operating procedures for all units

5. The one of the following which is MOST likely to occur in an over-specialized administrative set-up is   5.____
    A. inability to recruit proper personnel to fill over-specialized positions
    B. improper supervision
    C. failure of employees to realize the broad implications of their work

D. lack of proper decentralization of authority, as emphasis on specialization goes hand-in-hand with over-centralization
E. inability to solve technical problems which are not entirely in one specialty

6. Of the following, the LEAST valid reason for a department head continuing to require that a weekly report be forwarded to him, is that the report forms a basis for
   A. measuring performance
   B. making decisions
   C. revising policy
   D. the execution of the mission of the unit which receives it
   E. the operation of the unit which is required to prepare it

7. Administrators must learn not to farm out essential functions to unintegrated agencies, but to organize all responsibilities in unified but decentralized hierarchies.
   A problem which an administrator may be expected to face if he has not learned this is that
   A. the organization fails to develop administrators capable of independent action
   B. issues will not be posed at the level where decisions should be made
   C. relationships with the public will not be satisfactory
   D. it will be difficult to achieve administrative control or get agreement on departmental action
   E. individual agencies will be unable to complete the work scheduled

8. The central staff planning unit within any organization includes in its functions helping to plan policy at one extreme and planning detailed execution at the other extreme.
   With respect to the actual execution, the planning activity should
   A. have no concern with it
   B. simply forward and explain new plans
   C. have only the responsibility of explaining in the form of plans the objectives of top management
   D. keep track of how the plans are working out but make no attempt to supervise their execution
   E. supervise the execution of new plans

9. The head of a department assigned final responsibility for the training function to the personnel office.
   This assignment was
   A. *undesirable*; this type of centralization prevents a staff organization from carrying out staff functions
   B. *desirable*; experience has shown that centralization of this type results in more efficient and economic operation
   C. *undesirable*; the personnel office usually does not have the technical "know how" to carry this responsibility
   D. *desirable*; if training is left to the line officials, it never is accomplished
   E. *undesirable*; this responsibility must rest with the supervisor

3 (#3)

10. A department head insisted that operating officials participate in the development of new procedures along with the planning section.
    Participation of this type is, on the whole,
    A. *desirable*; operating realities are more likely to be considered
    B. *undesirable*; the inclusion of conflicting views before the plan is drawn may result in no plan
    C. *desirable*; plans will be more flexible and objectives more clearly defined
    D. *undesirable*; the operating officials should decide to what extent they wish to participate with no pressure from the top
    E. *desirable*; to back down on a procedure once it has been decided upon is a sign of weakness

10.____

11. Much of the current criticism of the administration of large organizations is basically a criticism of our failure to place the same emphasis on accountability that we do on authority and responsibility.
    The one of the following acts which is MOST likely to insure accountability for the discharge of responsibilities inherent in the delegation of authority is the
    A. establishment of appropriate reports and controls
    B. organization of a methods analysis section
    C. delegation of authority so made as to support functional or homogeneous activities
    D. delegation of authority so made as to preserve unity of command
    E. decentralization of responsibility and authority

11.____

12. This statement has been made:
    A man who is a top-notch executive in one organization would make a top-notch executive in any other organization, even if the organizations are as diverse as a sales agency and a research foundation.
    This statement is, in general,
    A. *correct*; the characteristics required for a good executive are invariant with respect to organization
    B. *incorrect*; there is no way of predicting how a good executive in one organization would be in any other
    C. *correct*; while the characteristics required for a good executive vary from organization to organization, the common core requirements are great enough to insure similar performance
    D. *incorrect*; although some prediction can be made, different types of organizations require different types of executives
    E. *correct*; success as an executive does not depend upon "characteristics" but on the man; if he is able to direct and execute in one organization he will be able to do so in any other

12.____

13. Reported information is not needed at levels higher than those at which decisions are made on the basis of the information reported.
    This statement is, in general,
    A. *correct*; if no action is to be taken on the basis of the information, the information is unnecessary
    B. *incorrect*; all information is of importance in arriving at a sound decision

13.____

C. *correct*; levels below the one at which the decision is made have need of the information
D. *incorrect*; levels below the one at which the decision is made do not have need of the information
E. *correct*; decisions should be made on the basis of information reported

14. Of the following, the characteristic of an organization which BEST shows that the organizational hierarchy is effective is that
    A. the department head commands the respect of the employees
    B. the organization is sufficiently flexible to assume functions in fields not related to his major field of endeavor
    C. responsibility has been appropriately delegated throughout the organization
    D. the department continues to function effectively even though there is continual turnover in the higher supervisory ranks
    E. no employee in the organization is subject to orders from more than one source

15. It is only because the primary purpose of traditional discipline has been to preserve the structure of command that a need has arisen for ameliorative safeguards such as a formal statement of "cause," right of hearing, and right of appeal.
    The BEST current practice with respect to discipline is that
    A. few ameliorative safeguards of the kind enumerated are desirable as their presence hurts the public service
    B. discipline is a means of controlling deviations from established authority
    C. the safeguards enumerated are not sufficient for the protection of the employee
    D. discipline should be based upon education, persuasion, and consultation
    E. unquestioned obedience to each order should not be expected but that a supervisor should be prepared at all times to demonstrate the reasonableness of his requests

16. Of the following types of work, the one for which a manual process is MOST usually to be preferred over a mechanized process is one in which the transactions are very
    A. numerous   B. similar   C. dissimilar
    D. predictable E. unpredictable

17. Work flow charts are used in an organization PRIMARILY because they
    A. indicate present and future objectives clearly
    B. are frequently used records
    C. clearly indicate when each operation will be performed
    D. summarize the work procedures of the organization
    E. tend to clarify thinking by presenting certain facts clearly

18. With respect to a report prepared by an IBM installation, the one of the following changes which is LEAST likely to cause a change in the procedure for preparing the report is a change in the
    A. volume of work
    B. source documents
    C. final report
    D. employees assigned
    E. time allowed for the preparation of the report

19. The one of the following which is NOT necessarily a characteristic of a good buying procedure is that it
    A. provides for proper analysis of purchases made
    B. is simple
    C. makes provision for substitutions where possible and necessary
    D. makes sealed bids mandatory
    E. recruits many bidders

20. Data relating to the operation of any unit should be accumulated and periodically summarized and analyzed PRIMARILY in order to
    A. point out the most efficient and least efficient workers
    B. determine the relative value of each procedure
    C. locate the elements of an operation which are unusually efficient or inefficient
    D. evaluate the importance of maintaining operating records and quotas
    E. compare the work performed by comparable units

21. Of the following, the MAJOR function of an administrative planning and research staff units is to
    A. investigate trouble points in the organization
    B. reorganize inefficient units
    C. assist the executive to plan future operations
    D. conduct continuous investigations and planning
    E. write the necessary operation and procedure manuals

22. The one of the following which does NOT require definition when setting up a work measurement system is the
    A. level of work accomplishment at which to measure
    B. work unit in which to measure
    C. time unit by which to measure
    D. acceptable quota for each activity
    E. reporting system to be used

23. During a discussion of the time unit that would be appropriate to measure employee-time in a work measurement program in a public agency, the man-day was suggested.
    This unit is
    A. *satisfactory*; record keeping will be kept to a minimum
    B. *unsatisfactory*; it will be difficult to verify the unit against official time records

C. *satisfactory*; it will be easy to verify the unit against official time records
D. *unsatisfactory*; its use will unnecessarily complicate record keeping
E. *satisfactory*; it permits more meaningful comparisons to be made between equal periods of time

24. As part of a space layout survey, an administrator instructed his subordinates to study the flow of work and sequence of operating procedures.
His MAJOR purposes in doing this was to determine
    A. the physical distribution and movement of personnel, material, and equipment
    B. the amount of space which is available and the amount of space which will be required
    C. the order in which the component steps in the different procedures are performed
    D. what future requirements will be, based on observable present trend
    E. how the distribution of personnel to various organization units is related to their space requirements

25. Before discussing a proposed office layout, the administrative officer stated, *"We intend to have a minimum number of private offices. We will assign private offices only where quiet is deemed essential or confidential conferences are required."*
The one of the following which is usually the MOST valid reason for this rule is that it
    A. permits proper placing of employees who deal with the public
    B. makes it easier to locate supervisors near the units they control
    C. tends to ensure that the work of each unit will flow continually forward within itself
    D. allows placing complementary units close together
    E. makes clerical supervision easier

KEY (CORRECT ANSWERS)

1.	D		11.	A
2.	C		12.	D
3.	E		13.	A
4.	A		14.	C
5.	C		15.	D
6.	E		16.	C
7.	D		17.	E
8.	D		18.	D
9.	E		19.	D
10.	A		20.	C

21. D
22. D
23. D
24. A
25. E

EXAMINATION SECTION
TEST 1

DIRECTIONS: Each question or incomplete statement is followed by several suggested answers or completions. Select the one that BEST answers the question or completes the statement. *PRINT THE LETTER OF THE CORRECT ANSWER IN THE SPACE AT THE RIGHT.*

1. An administrator in a department should be thoroughly familiar with modern methods of personnel administration.
   This statement is
   A. *true*, because this familiarity will help him in performing the normal functions of his office
   B. *false*, because personnel administration is not a departmental matter, but is centralized in the Civil Service Commission
   C. *true*, because this knowledge will insure the elimination of personnel problems in the department
   D. *false*, because departmental problems of a minor character are handled by the personnel representative, while major problems are the responsibility of the commissioner

   1.____

2. The LEAST true of the following is that an administrative assistant in a department
   A. executes the policy laid down by the commissioner or his deputies
   B. in the main, carries out the policies of the commissioner but with some leeway where his own frame of reference is determinative
   C. is never required to formulate policy
   D. is responsible for the successful accomplishment of a section of the department's program

   2.____

3. If a representative committee of employees in a large department is to meet with an administrative officer for the purpose of improve staff relations and of handling grievances, it is BEST that these meetings be held
   A. at regular intervals
   B. whenever requested by an aggrieved employee
   C. at the discretion of the administrative officer
   D. whenever the need arises

   3.____

4. In the theory and practice of public administration, the one of the following which is LEAST generally regarded as a staff function is
   A. budgeting   B. firefighting
   C. purchasing   D. research and information

   4.____

5. The LEAST essential factor in the successful application of a service rating system is
   A. careful training of reporting officers
   B. provision for self-rating
   C. statistical analysis to check reliability
   D. utilization of objective standards of performance

6. Of the following, the one which is NOT an aim of service rating plans is
   A. establishment of a fair method of measuring employee value to the employer
   B. application of a uniform measurement to employees of the same class and grade performing similar functions
   C. application of a uniform measurement to employees of the same class and grade however different their assignments may be
   D. establishment of a scientific duties plan

7. A rule or regulation relating to the internal management of a department becomes effective
   A. only after it is filed in the office of the clerk
   B. as soon as issued by the department head
   C. only after it has been published officially
   D. when approved by the mayor

8. Of the following, the one MOST generally regarded as an *administrative* power is the
   A. veto power
   B. message power
   C. power of pardon
   D. rule making power

9. In public administration functional allocation involves
   A. integration and the assignment of administrative power
   B. the assignment of a single power to a single administrative level
   C. the distribution of a number of subsidiary responsibilities among all levels of government
   D. decentralization of administrative responsibilities

10. In the field of public administration, the LEAST general result of coordination is the
    A. performance of a well-rounded job
    B. elimination of jurisdictional overlapping
    C. performance of functions otherwise neglected
    D. elimination of duplication of work

11. Of the following, the MOST complicated and difficult problem confronting the reorganizer in the field of public administration is
    A. ridding the government of graft
    B. ridding the government of crude incompetence
    C. ridding the government of excessive decentralization
    D. conditioning organization to modern social and economic life

12. The MOST accurate description of the process of integration in the field of public administration is
    A. transfer of administrative authority from a lower to a higher level of government
    B. transfer of administrative authority from a higher to a lower level of government
    C. concentration of administrative authority within one level of government
    D. formal cooperation between city and state governments to administer a function

13. The one of the following who was MOST closely allied with *scientific management* is
    A. Mosher B. Probst C. Taylor D. White

14. Of the following wall colors, the one which will reflect the GREATEST amount of light, other things being equal, is
    A. buff B. light gray C. light blue D. brown

15. Natural illumination is LEAST necessary in a(n)
    A. executive office
    B. reception room
    C. central stenographic bureau
    D. conference room

16. The MOST desirable relative humidity in an office is
    A. 30% B. 50% c. 70% D. 90%

17. When several pieces of correspondence are filed in the same folder, they are USUALLY arranged
    A. according to subject
    B. numerically
    C. in the order in which they are received
    D. alphabetically

18. Eliminating slack in work assignment is
    A. speed-up
    B. time study
    C. motion study
    D. efficient management

19. *Time studies* examine and measure
    A. past performance
    B. present performance
    C. long-run effect
    D. influence of change

20. In making a position analysis for a duties classification, the one of the following factors which must be considered is the _____ the incumbent.
    A. capabilities of
    B. qualifications of
    C. efficiency attained by
    D. responsibility assigned to

21. The MAXIMUM number of subordinates who can be effectively supervised by one administrative assistant is BEST considered as
    A. determined by the law of *span of control*
    B. determined by the law of *span of attention*
    C. determined by the type of work supervised
    D. fixed at not more than six

21.____

22. Of the following devices used in personnel administration, the MOST basic is
    A. classification
    B. service rating
    C. appeals
    D. in-service training

22.____

23. Of the following, the LEAST important factor for sound organization is the
    A. individual and his position
    B. hierarchical form of organization
    C. location and delegation of authority
    D. standardization of salary schedules

23.____

24. *Stretch-out* is a term that originated with the
    A. imposition of a furlough
    B. system of semi-monthly relief payments
    C. development of labor technology
    D. irregular development of low-cost housing projects

24.____

25. The one of the following which is LEAST generally true of a personnel division in a large department is that it is
    A. concerned with having a certain point of view on personnel permeate the executive staff
    B. charged with aiding operating executives with auxiliary staff service, assistance and advice
    C. charged to administer a certain few operating duties of its own
    D. charged with the basic responsibility for the efficient operation of the entire department

25.____

KEY (CORRECT ANSWERS)

1.	A	11.	D
2.	C	12.	C
3.	A	13.	C
4.	B	14.	A
5.	B	15.	B
6.	D	16.	A
7.	B	17.	C
8.	D	18.	D
9.	C	19.	B
10.	C	20.	D

21. C
22. A
23. D
24. C
25. D

TEST 2

DIRECTIONS: Each question or incomplete statement is followed by several suggested answers or completions. Select the one that BEST answers the question or completes the statement. *PRINT THE LETTER OF THE CORRECT ANSWER IN THE SPACE AT THE RIGHT.*

Questions 1-10.

DIRECTIONS: Below are ten words numbered 1 through 10 and twenty other words divided into four groups—Group A, Group B, Group C, and Group D. For each of the ten numbered words, select the word in one of the four groups which is MOST NEARLY the same in meaning. The letter of that group is the answer for the item.

GROUP A	GROUP B	GROUP C	GROUP D
articulation	bituminous	assumption	scope
fusion	deductive	forecast	vindication
catastrophic	repudiation	terse	amortization
inductive	doleful	insolence	productive
leadership	prolonged	panorama	slanderous

1. abnegation   1._____

2. calumnious   2._____

3. purview   3._____

4. lugubrious   4._____

5. hegemony   5._____

6. arrogation   6._____

7. coalescence   7._____

8. prolix   8._____

9. syllogistic   9._____

10. contumely   10._____

11. In large cities the total cost of government is of course GREATER than in small cities but   11._____
    A. this is accompanied by a decrease in per capita cost
    B. the per capita cost is also greater
    C. the per capita cost is approximately the same
    D. the per capita cost is considerably less in approximately 50% of the cases

12. The one of the following which is LEAST characteristic of governmental reorganizations is the
    A. saving of large sums of money
    B. problem of morale and personnel
    C. task of logic and management
    D. engineering approach

13. The LEAST accurate of the following statements about graphic presentation is
    A. it is desirable to show as many coordinate lines as possible in a finished diagram
    B. the horizontal scale should read from left to right and the vertical scale from top to bottom
    C. when two or more curves are represented for comparison on the same chart, their zero lines should coincide
    D. a percentage curve should not be used when the purpose is to show the actual amounts of increase or decrease

14. Grouping of figures in a frequency distribution results in a *loss* of
    A. linearity   B. significance   C. detail   D. coherence

15. The true financial condition of a city is BEST reflected when its accounting system is placed upon a(n) _____ basis.
    A. cash   B. accrual   C. fiscal   D. warrant

16. When the discrepancy between the totals of a trial balance is $36, the LEAST probable cause of the error is
    A. omission of an item
    B. entering of an item on the wrong side of the ledger
    C. a mistake in addition or subtraction
    D. transposition of digits

17. For the MOST effective administrative management, appropriations should be
    A. itemized
    B. lump sum
    C. annual
    D. bi-annual

18. Of the following types of expenditure control in the practice of fiscal management, the one which is LEAST important is that which relates to
    A. past policy affecting expenditures
    B. future policy affecting expenditures
    C. prevention of improper use of funds
    D. prevention of overdraft

19. The sinking fund method of retiring bonds does NOT
    A. permit investment in a new issue of city bonds when the general market is unsatisfactory
    B. cause irreparable injury to the city's credit when the city is unable to make a scheduled contribution
    C. require periodic actuarial computations
    D. cost as much to administer as the serial bond method

20. Of the following, the statement that is FALSE is:
    A. Non-profit hospitalization plans are based on underlying principles similar to those which underlie mutual insurance.
    B. Federal, state, and local governments pay for more than half of the medical care received by more than half of the population of the country.
    C. In addition to non-profit hospitalization, non-profit organizations providing reimbursement for medical and nursing care are now being organized in this state.
    D. Voluntary health insurance must be depended on since a state system of health insurance is unconstitutional.

21. The MOST accurate of the following statements concerning birth and death rates is:
    A. A high birth rate is usually accompanied by a relatively high death rate.
    B. A high birth rate is usually accompanied by a relatively low death rate.
    C. The rate of increase in population for a given area may be obtained by subtracting the death rate from the birth rate.
    D. The rate of increase in population for a given area may be obtained by subtracting the birth rate from the death rate.

22. Empirical reasoning is based upon
    A. experience and observation
    B. *a priori* propositions
    C. application of an established generalization
    D. logical deduction

23. 45% of the employees of a certain department are enrolled in in-service training courses and 35% are registered in college courses.
    The percentage of employees NOT enrolled in either of these types of courses is
    A. 20%
    B. at least 20% and not more than 55%
    C. approximately 40%
    D. none of the above

24. A typist can address approximately R envelopes in a 7-hour day. A list containing S addresses is submitted with a request that all envelopes be typed within T hours.
    The number of typists needed to complete this task would b
    A. $\dfrac{7RS}{T}$
    B. $\dfrac{S}{7RT}$
    C. $\dfrac{R}{7ST}$
    D. $\dfrac{7S}{RT}$

4 (#2)

25. Bank X allows a customer to write without charge five checks per month for each $100 on deposit, but a check deposited or a cash deposit counts the same as a check written. Bank Y charges ten cents for every check written, requires no minimum balance and allows deposit of cash or of checks made out to customer free. A man receives two salary checks and, on the average, five other checks each month. He pays, on the average, twelve bills a month, five of which are for amounts between $5 and $10, five for amounts between $10 and $20, two for about $30. Assume that he pays these bills either by check or by Post Office money order (the charges for money orders are: $3.01 to $10-11¢; $10.01 to $20-13¢; $20.01 to $40-15¢) and that he has a savings account paying 2%. Assume also that if he has an account at Bank X, he keeps a balance sufficient to avoid any service charges.
Of the following statements in relation to this man, the one that is TRUE is that
   A. the monthly cost of an account at Bank Y is approximately as great as the cost of an account at Bank X and also the account is more convenient
   B. to use an account at Bank Y costs more than the use of money orders, but this disadvantage is offset by the fact that cancelled checks act as receipts for bills paid
   C. money orders are cheapest but this advantage is offset by the fact that one must go to the Post Office for each order
   D. an account at Bank X is least expensive and has the advantage that checks endorsed to the customer may be deposited in it

25.____

KEY (CORRECT ANSWERS)

1.	B		11.	B
2.	D		12.	A
3.	D		13.	A
4.	B		14.	C
5.	A		15.	B
6.	C		16.	C
7.	A		17.	B
8.	B		18.	A
9.	B		19.	B
10.	C		20.	D

21. A
22. A
23. B
24. D
25. D

EXAMINATION SECTION
TEST 1

DIRECTIONS: Each question or incomplete statement is followed by several suggested answers or completions. Select the one that BEST answers the question or completes the statement. *PRINT THE LETTER OF THE CORRECT ANSWER IN THE SPACE AT THE RIGHT.*

1. An executive assigns A, the head of a staff unit, to devise plans for reducing the delay in submittal of reports by a local agency headed by C. The reports are under the supervision of C's subordinate line official B with whom A is to deal directly. In his investigation, A finds: (1) the reasons for the delay; and (2) poor practices which have either been overlooked or condoned by line official B.
   Of the following courses of action A could take, the BEST one would be to
   A. develop recommendations with line official B with regard to reducing the delay and correcting the poor practice and then report fully to his own executive
   B. discuss the findings with C in an attempt to correct the situation before making any formal report on the poor practices
   C. report both findings to his executive, attaching the explanation offered by C
   D. report to his executive on the first finding and discuss the second in a friendly way with line official B
   E. report the first finding to his executive, ignoring the second until his opinion is requested

1.____

2. Drafts of a proposed policy, prepared by a staff committee, are circulated to ten member of the field staff of the organization by route slips with a request for comments within two weeks. Two members of the field staff make extensive comments, four offer editorial suggestions, and the remainder make minor favorable comments. Shortly after, it found that the statement needs considerable revision by the field staff.
   Of the following possible reasons for the original failure of the field staff to identify difficulties, the MOST likely is that the
   A. field staff did not take sufficient time to review the manual
   B. field staff had not been advised of the type of contribution expected
   C. low morale of the field staff prevented their showing interest
   D. policy statement was too advanced for the staff
   E. staff committee was not sufficiently representative

2.____

3. Operator participation in management improvement work is LEAST likely to
   A. assure the use of best available management technique
   B. overcome the stigma of the outside expert
   C. place responsibility for improvement in the person who knows the job best
   D. simplify installation
   E. take advantage of the desire of most operators to seek self-improvement

3.____

4. In general, the morale of workers in an agency is MOST frequently and MOST significantly affected by the
   A. agency policies of organizational structure and operational procedures
   B. distance of the employee's job from his home community
   C. fringe benefits
   D. number of opportunities for advancement
   E. relationship with supervisors

5. Of the following, the PRIMARY function of a work distribution chart is to
   A. analyze the soundness of existing divisions of labor
   B. eliminate the unnecessary clerical detail
   C. establish better supervisory techniques
   D. simplify work methods
   E. weed out core functions

6. In analyzing a process chart, which one of the following should be asked FIRST?
   A. How   B. When   C. Where   D. Who   E. Why

7. Which one of the following is NOT an advantage of the interview method of collecting data? It
   A. enables interviewer to judge the person interviewed on such matters as general attitude, knowledge, etc.
   B. helps build up personal relations for later installation of changes
   C. is a flexible method that can be adjusted to changing circumstances
   D. permits the obtaining of *off the record* information
   E. produces more accurate information than other methods

8. Which one of the following may be defined as a *regularly recurring appraisal of the manner in which all elements of agency management are being carried out*?
   A. Functional survey   B. Operations audit
   C. Organization survey   D. Over-all survey
   E. Reconnaissance survey

9. An analysis of the flow of work in a department should begin with the _____ work.
   A. major routine   B. minor routine   C. supervisory
   D. technical   E. unusual

10. Which method would MOST likely be used to get first-hand information on complaints from the public?
    A. Study of correspondence
    B. Study of work volume
    C. Tracing specific transactions through a series of steps
    D. Tracing use of forms
    E. Worker desk audit

11. People will generally produce the MOST if   11.____
    A. management exercises close supervision over the work
    B. there is strict discipline in the group
    C. they are happy in their work
    D. they feel involved in their work
    E. they follow *the one best way*

12. The normal analysis of which chart listed below is MOST closely related to   12.____
    organizational analysis? _____ chart.
    A. Layout   B. Operation   C. Process
    D. Work count   E. Work distribution

13. The work count would be LEAST helpful in accomplishing which one of the   13.____
    following?
    A. Demonstrating personnel needs   B. Improving the sequence of steps
    C. Measuring the value of a step   D. Spotting bottlenecks
    E. Stimulating interest in work

14. Which one of the following seems LEAST useful as a guide in interviewing   14.____
    an employee in a procedure and methods survey?
    A. Explaining who you are and the purpose of your visit
    B. Having a general plan of what you intend to get from the interview
    C. Listening carefully and not interrupting
    D. Trying out his reactions to your ideas for improvements
    E. Trying to analyze his reasons for saying what he says

15. Which one of the following is an advantage of the questionnaire method of   15.____
    gathering facts as compared with the interview method?
    A. Different people may interpret the questions differently
    B. Less *off the record* information is given
    C. More time may be taken in order to give exact answers
    D. Personal relationships with the people involved are not established
    E. There is less need for follow-up

16. Which one of the following is generally NOT an advantage of the personal   16.____
    observation method of gathering facts? It
    A. enables staff to use *off the record* information if personally observed
    B. helps in developing valid recommendations
    C. helps the person making the observation acquire *know how* valuable for
       later installation and follow-up
    D. is economical in time and money
    E. may turn up other problems in need of solution

17. Which of the following would MOST often be the best way to minimize   17.____
    resistance to change?
    A. Break the news about the change gently to the people affected
    B. Increase the salary of the people affected by the change
    C. Let the people concerned participate at the decision to change

D. Notify all people concerned with the change, both orally and in writing
E. Stress the advantages of the new system

18. The functional organization chart
    A. does not require periodic revision
    B. includes a description of the duties of each organization segment
    C. includes positions and titles for each organization segment
    D. is the simplest type of organization chart
    E. is used primarily by newly established agencies

    18.____

19. The principle of span of control has frequently been said to be in conflict with the
    A. principle of unity of command
    B. principle that authority should be commensurate with responsibility
    C. principle that like functions should be grouped into one unit
    D. principle that the number of levels between the top of an organization and the bottom should be small
    E. scalar principle

    19.____

20. If an executive delegates to his subordinates authority to handle problems of a routine nature for which standard solutions have been established, he may expect that
    A. fewer complaint will be received
    B. he has made it more difficult for his subordinates to solve these problems
    C. he has opened the way for confusion in his organization
    D. there will be a lack of consistency in the methods applied to the solution of these problems
    E. these routine problems will be handled efficiently and he will have more time for other non-routine work

    20.____

21. Which of the following would MOST likely be achieved by a change in the basic organization structure from the *process* or *functional* type to the *purpose* or *product* type?
    A. Easier recruitment of personnel in a tight labor market
    B. Fixing responsibility at a lower level in the organization
    C. Greater centralization
    D. Greater economy
    E. Greater professional development

    21.____

22. Usually the MOST difficult problem in connection with a major reorganization is
    A. adopting a pay plan to fit the new structure
    B. bringing the organization manual up-to-date
    C. determining the new organization structure
    D. gaining acceptance of the new plan by the higher level employees
    E. gaining acceptance of the new plan by the lower level employees

    22.____

23. Which of the following statements MOST accurately describes the work of the chiefs of MOST staff divisions in departments?
Chiefs
    A. focus more on getting the job done than on how it is done
    B. are mostly interested in short-range results
    C. nearly always advise but rarely advise
    D. usually command or control but rarely advise
    E. provide service to the rest of the organization and/or assist the chief executive in planning and controlling operations

23.____

24. In determining the type of organization structure of an enterprise, the one factor that might be given relatively greater weight in a small organization than in a larger organization of the same nature is the
    A. geographical location of the enterprise
    B. individual capabilities of incumbents
    C. method of financing to be employed
    D. size of the area served
    E. type of activity engaged in

24.____

25. Functional foremanship differs MOST markedly from generally accepted principle of administration in that it advocates
    A. an unlimited span of control
    B. less delegation of responsibility
    C. more than one supervisor for an employee
    D. nonfunctional organization
    E. substitution of execution for planning

25.____

KEY (CORRECT ANSWERS)

1.	A	11.	D
2.	B	12.	E
3.	A	13.	B
4.	E	14.	D
5.	A	15.	C
6.	E	16.	D
7.	E	17.	C
8.	B	18.	B
9.	A	19.	D
10.	A	20.	E

21.	B
22.	D
23.	E
24.	B
25.	C

TEST 2

DIRECTIONS: Each question or incomplete statement is followed by several suggested answers or completions. Select the one that BEST answers the question or completes the statement. *PRINT THE LETTER OF THE CORRECT ANSWER IN THE SPACE AT THE RIGHT.*

1. Decentralization of the authority to make decisions is a necessary result of increased complexity in an organization, but for the sake of efficiency and coordination of operations, such decentralization must be planned carefully. A good general rule is that
   A. any decision should be made at the lowest possible point in the organization where all the information and competence necessary for a sound decision are available
   B. any decision should be made at the highest possible point in the organization, thus guaranteeing the best decision
   C. any decision should be made at the lowest possible point in the organization, but always approved by management
   D. any decision should be made by management and referred to the proper subordinate for comment
   E. no decision should be made by any individual in the organization without approval by a superior

1._____

2. One drawback of converting a conventional consecutive filing system to a terminal digit filing system for a large installation is that
   A. conversion would be expensive in time and manpower
   B. conversion would prevent the proper use of recognized numeric classification systems, such as the Dewey decimal, in classifying files material
   C. responsibility for proper filing cannot be pinpointed in the terminal digit system
   D. the terminal digit system requires considerably more space than a normal filing system

2._____

3. The basic filing system that would ordinarily be employed in a large administrative headquarters unit is the _____ file system.
   A alphabetic   B. chronological
   C. mnemonic   D. retention
   E. subject classification

3._____

4. A records center is of benefit in a records management program PRIMARILY because
   A. all the records of the organization are kept in one place
   B. inactive records can be stored economically in less expense storage areas
   C. it provides a place where useless records can be housed at little or no cost to the organization

4._____

2 (#2)

    D. obsolete filing and storage equipment can be utilized out of view of the public
    E. records analysts can examine an organization's files without affecting the unit's operation or upsetting the supervisors

5. In examining a number of different forms to see whether any could be combined or eliminated, which of the following would one be MOST likely to use?
    A. Forms analysis sheet of recurring data
    B. Forms control log
    C. Forms design and approval request
    D. Forms design and guide sheet
    E. Numerical file

5.____

6. The MOST important reason for control of *bootleg* forms is that
    A. they are more expensive than authorized forms
    B. they are usually poorly designed
    C. they can lead to unnecessary procedures
    D. they cannot be reordered as easily as authorized terms
    E. violation of rules and regulations should not be allowed

6.____

7. With a box design of a form, the caption title or question to be answered should be located in the _____ of the box.
    A. center at the bottom   B. center at the top
    C. lower left corner   D. lower right corner
    E. upper left corner

7.____

8. A two-part snapout form would be MOST properly justified if
    A. it is a cleaner operation
    B. it is prepared ten times a week
    C. it saves time in preparation
    D. it is to be filled out by hand rather than by typewriter
    E. proper registration is critical

8.____

9. When deciding whether or not to approve a request for a new form, which reference is normally MOST pertinent?
    A. Alphabetical Forms File   B. Functional Forms File
    C. Numerical Forms File   D. Project Completion Report
    E. Records Retention Data

9.____

10. Which of the following statements BEST explains the significance of the famed Hawthorne Plant experiments?
They showed that
    A. a large span of control leads to more production than a small span of control
    B. morale has no relationship to production
    C. personnel counseling is of relatively little importance in a going organization

10.____

D. the special attention received by a group in an experimental situation has a greater impact on production than changes in working conditions
E. there is a direct relationship between the amount of illumination and production

11. Which of the following would most often NOT result from a highly efficient management control system?
    A. Facilitation of delegation
    B. Highlighting of problem areas
    C. Increase in willingness of people to experiment or to take calculated risks
    D. Provision of an objective test of new ideas or new methods and procedures
    E. Provision of information useful for revising objectives, programs, and operations

12. The PERT system is a
    A. method for laying out office space on a modular basis utilizing prefabricated partitions
    B. method of motivating personnel to be continuously alert and to improve their appearance
    C. method of program planning and control using a network or flow plan
    D. plan for expanding reporting techniques
    E. simplified method of cost accounting

13. The term *management control* is MOST frequently used to mean
    A. an objective and unemotional approach by management
    B. coordinating the efforts of all parts of the organization
    C. evaluation of results in relation to plan
    D. giving clear, precise orders to subordinates
    E. keeping unions from making managerial decisions

14. Which one of the following factors has the MOST bearing on the frequency with which a control report should be made?
    A. Degree of specialization of the work
    B. Degree of variability in activities
    C. Expense of the report
    D. Number of levels of supervision
    E. Number of personnel involved

15. The value of statistical records is MAINLY dependent upon the
    A. method of presenting the material
    B. number of items used
    C. range of cases sampled
    D. reliability of the information used
    E. time devoted to compiling the material

16. When a supervisor delegates an assignment, he should
    A. delegate his responsibility for the assignment
    B. make certain that the assignment is properly performed
    C. participate in the beginning and final stages of the assignment
    D. retail all authority needed to complete the assignment
    E. oversee all stages of the assignment

17. Assume that the department in which you are employed has never given official sanction to a mid-afternoon coffee break. Some bureaus have it and others do not. In the latter case, some individuals merely absent themselves for about 15 minutes at 3 P.M. while others remain on the job despite the fatigue which seems to be common among all employees in this department at that time.
    The course of action which you should recommend, if possible, is to
    A. arrange a schedule of mid-afternoon coffee breaks for all employees
    B. forbid all employees to take a mid-afternoon coffee break
    C. permit each bureau to decide for itself whether or not it will have a coffee break
    D. require all employees who wish a coffee break to take a shorter lunch period
    E. arrange a poll to discover the consensus of the department

18. The one of the following which is LEAST important in the management of a suggestion program is
    A. giving awards which are of sufficient value to encourage competition
    B. securing full support from the department's officers and executives
    C. publicizing the program and the awards given
    D. holding special conferences to analyze and evaluate some of the suggestions needed
    E. providing suggestion boxes in numerous locations

19. The one of the following which is MOST likely to decrease morale is
    A. insistence on strict adherence to safety rules
    B. making each employee responsible for the tidiness of his work area
    C. overlooking evidence of hostility between groups of employees
    D. strong, aggressive leadership
    E. allocating work on the basis of personal knowledge of the abilities and interests of the member of the department

20. Assume that a certain office procedure has been standard practice for many years.
    When a new employee asks why this particular procedure is followed, the supervisor should FIRST
    A. explain that everyone does it that way
    B. explain the reason for the procedure
    C. inform him that it has always been done that way in that particular office
    D. tell him to try it for a while before asking questions
    E. tell him he has never thought about it that way

21. Several employees complain informally to their supervisor regarding some new procedures which have been instituted.
The supervisor should IMMEDIATELY
    A. explain that management is responsible
    B. state frankly that he had nothing to do with it
    C. refer the matter to the methods analyst
    D. tell the employees to submit their complaint as a formal grievance
    E. investigate the complaint

22. A new employee asks his supervisor how he is doing. Actually, he is not doing well in some phases of the job, but it is felt that he will learn in time.
The BEST response for the supervisor to make is:
    A. Some things you are doing well, and in others I am sure you will improve.
    B. Wait until the end of your probation period when we will discuss this matter.
    C. You are not doing too well.
    D. You are doing very well.
    E. I'll be able to tell you when I go over your record.

23. The PRINCIPAL aim of a supervisor is to
    A. act as liaison between employee and management
    B. get the work done
    C. keep up morale
    D. train his subordinates
    E. become chief of the department

24. When the work of two bureaus must be coordinated, direct contact between the subordinates in each bureau who are working on the problem is
    A. *bad*, because it violates the chain of command
    B. *bad*, because they do not have authority to make decisions
    C. *good*, because it enable quicker results
    D. *good*, because it relieves their superiors of any responsibilities
    E. *bad*, because they may work at cross purposes

25. Of the following, the organization defect which can be ascertained MOST readily merely by analyzing an accurate and well-drawn organization chart is
    A. ineffectiveness of an activity
    B. improper span of control
    C. inappropriate assignment of functions
    D. poor supervision
    E. unlawful delegation of authority

KEY (CORRECT ANSWERS)

1. A
2. A
3. E
4. B
5. A

6. C
7. E
8. E
9. B
10. D

11. C
12. C
13. C
14. B
15. D

16. B
17. A
18. E
19. C
20. B

21. E
22. A
23. B
24. C
25. B

EXAMINATION SECTION
TEST 1

DIRECTIONS: Each question or incomplete statement is followed by several suggested answers or completions. Select the one that BEST answers the question or completes the statement. *PRINT THE LETTER OF THE CORRECT ANSWER IN THE SPACE AT THE RIGHT.*

1. It is often desirable for an administrator to consult, during the planning process, the persons to be affected by those plans.
   Of the following, the MAJOR justification for such consultation is that it recognizes the
   A. fact that participating in horizontal planning is almost always more effective than participating in vertical planning
   B. principle of participation and the need for a sense of belonging as a means of decreasing resistance and developing support
   C. principle that lower-level administrators normally are more likely than higher-level administrators to emphasize longer-range goals
   D. fact that final responsibility for the approval of plans should be placed in committees not individuals

   1.____

2. In evaluating performance and, if necessary, correcting what is being done to assure attainment of results according to plan, it is GENERALLY best for the administrator to do which one of the following?
   A. Make a continual effort to increase the number of written control reports prepared
   B. Thoroughly investigate in equal detail all possible deviations indicated by comparison of performance to expectation
   C. Decentralize, within an operating unit or division, the responsibility for correcting deviations
   D. Concentrate on the exceptions, or outstanding variations, from the expected results or standards

   2.____

3. Generally, changes in the ways in which the supervisors and employees in an organization do things are MORE likely to be welcomed by them when the changes
   A. threaten the security of the supervisors than when they do not
   B. are inaugurated after prior change has been assimilated than when they are inaugurated before other major changes have been assimilated
   C. follow a series of failures in changes when they follow a series of successful changes
   D. are dictated by personal order rather than when they result from an application of previously established impersonal principles

   3.____

4. For sound organization relationships, of the following, it is generally MOST desirable that
   A. authority and responsibility be segregated from each other, in order to facilitate control
   B. the authority of a manager should be commensurate with his responsibility, and vice versa
   C. authority be defined as the obligation of an individual to carry out assigned activities to the best of his or her ability
   D. clear recognition be given to the fact that delegation of authority benefits only the manager who delegates it

5. In utilizing a checklist of questions for general managerial planning, which one of the following generally is the FIRST question to be asked and answered?
   A. Where will it take place?
   B. How will it be done?
   C. Why must it be done?
   D. Who will do it?

6. Of the following, it is USUALLY best to set administrative objectives so that they are
   A. at a level that is unattainable, so that administrators will continually be strongly motivated
   B. at a level that is attainable, but requires some stretching and reaching by administrators trying to attain them
   C. stated in qualitative rather than quantitative terms whenever a choice between the two is possible
   D. stated in a general and unstructured manner, to permit each administrator maximum freedom in interpreting them

7. In selecting from among administrative alternatives, three general bases for decisions are open to the manager – experience, experimentation, and research and analysis. Of the following, the best argument AGAINST primary reliance upon experimentation as the method of evaluating administrative alternatives is that experimentation is
   A. generally the most expensive of the three techniques
   B. almost always legally prohibited in procedural matters
   C. possible only in areas where results may be easily duplicated by other experimenters at any time
   D. an approach that requires information on scientific method seldom available to administrators

8. The administrator who utilizes the techniques of operations research, linear programming and simulation in making an administrative decision should MOST appropriately be considered to be using the techniques of _____ analysis.
   A. intuitive   B. quantitative
   C. nonmathematical   D. qualitative

9. When an additional organizational level is added within a department, that department has MOST directly manifested
    A. horizontal growth
    B. horizontal shrinkage
    C. vertical growth
    D. vertical shrinkage

10. Of the following, the one which GENERALLY is the most intangible planning factor is
    A. budget dollars allocated to a function
    B. square feet of space for office use
    C. number of personnel in various clerical titles
    D. emotional impact of a proposed personnel policy among employees

11. Departmentation by function is the same as, or most similar to, departmentation by
    A. equipment
    B. clientele
    C. territory
    D. activity

12. Such verifiable factors as turnover, absenteeism or volume of grievances would generally BEST assist in measuring the effectiveness of a program to improve
    A. forms control
    B. employee morale
    C. linear programming
    D. executive creativity

13. An organization increases the number of subordinates reporting to a manager up to the point where incremental savings in costs, better communication and morale, and other factors equal incremental losses in effectiveness of control, direction and similar factors. This action MOST specifically employs the technique of
    A. role playing
    B. queuing theory
    C. marginal analysis
    D. capital standards analysis

14. The term *computer hardware* is MOST likely to refer to
    A. machines and equipment
    B. Ethernet and USB cables
    C. training manuals
    D. word processing and spreadsheet programs

15. Determining what is being accomplished, that is, evaluating the performance and, if necessary, applying corrective measures so that performance takes place according to plans is MOST appropriately called management
    A. actuating
    B. planning
    C. controlling
    D. motivating

16. Of the following, the BEST overall technique for choosing from among several alternative public programs proposed to try to achieve the same broad objective generally is _____ analysis.
    A. random-sample
    B. input
    C. cost-effectiveness
    D. output

17. When the success of a plan in achieving specific program objectives is measured against that plan's costs, the measure obtained is most directly that of the plan's
    A. pervasiveness
    B. control potential
    C. primacy
    D. efficiency

18. Generally, the degree to which an organization's planning will be coordinated varies MOST directly with the degree to which
    A. the individuals charged with executing plans are better compensated than those charged with developing and evaluating plans
    B. the individuals charged with planning understand and agree to utilize consistent planning premises
    C. a large number of position classification titles have been established for those individuals charged with organizational planning functions
    D. subordinate unit objectives are allowed to control the overall objectives of the departments of which such subordinate units are a part

19. The responsibility for specific types of decisions generally is BEST delegated to
    A. the highest organizational level at which there is an individual possessing the ability, desire, impartiality and access to relevant information needed to make these decisions
    B. the lowest organizational level at which there is an individual possessing the ability, desire, impartiality and access to relevant information needed to make these decisions
    C. a group of executives, rather than a single executive, if these decisions deal with an emergency
    D. the organizational level midway between that which will have to carry out these decisions and that which will have to authorize the resources for their implementation

20. The process of managing by objectives is MOST likely to lead to a situation in which the
    A. goal accomplishment objectives of managers tend to have a longer timespan as one goes lower down the line in an organization
    B. establishment of quantitative goals for staff positions is generally easier than the establishment of quantitative goals for line positions
    C. development of objectives requires the manager to think of the way he will accomplish given results, and of the organization, personnel and resources that he will need
    D. superiors normally develop and finally approve detailed goals for subordinates without any prior consultation with either those subordinates or with the top-level executives responsible for the longer-run objectives of the organization

21. As used with respect to decision making, the application of scientific method to the study of alternatives in a problem situation, with a view to providing a quantitative basis for arriving at an optimum solution in terms of the goals sought is MOST appropriately called
    A. simple number departmentation
    B. geographic decentralization
    C. operations research
    D. trait rating

21.____

22. Assume that a bureau head proposes that final responsibility and authority for all planning within the bureau is to be delegated to one employee who is to be paid at the level of an assistant division head in that bureau.
    Of the following, the MOST appropriate comment about this proposal is that it's
    A. *improper*, mainly because planning does not call for someone at such a high level
    B. *improper*, mainly because responsibility for a basic management function such as planning may not properly be delegated as proposed
    C. *proper*, mainly because ultimate responsibility for all bureau planning is best placed as proposed
    D. *proper*, mainly because every well-managed bureau should have a full-time planning officer

22.____

23. Of the following, the MOST important reason that participation has motivating effects is generally that it gives to the individual participating
    A. a recognition of his or her desire to feel important and to contribute to achievement of worthwhile goals
    B. an opportunity to participate in work that is beyond the scope of the class specification for his or her title
    C. a secure knowledge that his or her organization's top leadership is as efficient as possible considering all major circumstances
    D. the additional information likely to be crucial to his or her promotion

23.____

24. Of the following, the MOST essential characteristic of an effective employee suggestion system is that
    A. suggestions be submitted upward through the chain of command
    B. suggestions be acted upon promptly so that employees may be promptly informed of what happens to their submitted suggestions
    C. suggesters be required to sign their names on the material sent to the actual evaluators for evaluation
    D. suggesters receive at least 25% of the agency's savings during the first two years after their suggestions have been accepted and put into effect by the agency

24.____

25. Two organizations have the same basic objectives and the same total number of employees. The span of authority of each intermediate manager is narrower in one organization than it is in the other. It is MOST likely that the organization in which each intermediate manager has a narrower span of authority will have
    A. fewer intermediate managers
    B. more organizational levels
    C. more managers reporting to a larger number of intermediate supervisors
    D. more characteristics of a *flat* organizational structure

25._____

KEY (CORRECT ANSWERS)

1.	B	11.	D
2.	D	12.	B
3.	B	13.	C
4.	B	14.	A
5.	C	15.	C
6.	B	16.	C
7.	A	17.	D
8.	B	18.	B
9.	C	19.	B
10.	D	20.	C

21.	C
22.	B
23.	A
24.	B
25.	B

TEST 2

DIRECTIONS: Each question or incomplete statement is followed by several suggested answers or completions. Select the one that BEST answers the question or completes the statement. *PRINT THE LETTER OF THE CORRECT ANSWER IN THE SPACE AT THE RIGHT.*

1. Which one of the following BEST expresses the essence of the merit idea or system in public employment?
    A. A person's worth to the organization—the merit of his or her attributes and capacities—is the governing factor in his or her selection, assignment, pay, recognition, advancement and retention
    B. Written tests of the objective type are the only fair way to select on a merit basis from among candidates for open-competitive appointment to positions within the merit system
    C. Employees who have qualified for civil service positions shall have lifetime tenure during good behavior in those positions regardless of changes in public programs
    D. Periodic examinations with set date limits within which all persons desiring to demonstrate their merit may apply, shall be publicly advertised and held for all promotional titles

1.____

2. Of the following, the promotion selection policy generally considered MOST antithetical to the merit concept is the promotion selection policy which
    A. is based solely on objective tests of competence
    B. is based solely on seniority
    C. may require a manager to lose his or her best employee to another part of the organization
    D. permits operating managers collectively to play a significant role in promotion decisions

2.____

3. Of the following, the problems encountered by government establishments which are MOST likely to make extensive delegation of authority difficult to effectuate tend to be problems of
    A. accountability and ensuring uniform administration
    B. line and staff relationships within field offices
    C. generally employee opposition to such delegation of authority and to the subsequent record-keeping activities
    D. use of the management-by-objectives approach

3.____

4. The major decisions as to which jobs shall be created and who shall carry which responsibilities should GENERALLY be made by
    A. budgetary advisers
    B. line managers
    C. classification specialists
    D. peer-level rating committees

4.____

5. The ultimate controlling factor in structuring positions in the public service, MOST generally, should be the
   A. possibility of providing upgrading for highly productive employees
   B. collective bargaining demands initially made by established public employee unions
   C. positive motivational effects upon productivity resulting from an inverted pyramid job structure
   D. effectiveness of the structuring in serving the mission of the organization

6. Of the following, the most usual reason for unsatisfactory line-staff relationships is
   A. inept use of the abilities of staff personnel by line management
   B. the higher salaries paid to line officials
   C. excessive consultation between line officials and staff officials at the same organizational level
   D. a feeling among the staff members that only lower-level line members appreciate their work

7. Generally, an employee receiving new information from a fellow employee is MOST likely to
   A. forget the new information if it is consistent with his or her existing beliefs much more easily than he or she forgets the new information if it is inconsistent with existing beliefs
   B. accept the validity of the new information if it is consistent with his or her existing beliefs more readily than he or she accepts the validity of the new information if it is inconsistent with existing beliefs
   C. have a less accurate memory of the new information if it is consistent with his or her existing beliefs than he or she has of the new information if it is inconsistent with existing beliefs
   D. ignore the new information if it is consistent with his or her existing beliefs more often than he or she ignores the new information if it is inconsistent with existing beliefs

8. Virtually all of us use this principle in our human communications – perhaps without realizing it. In casual conversations, we are alert for cues to whether we are understood (e.g., attentive nods from the other person). Similarly, an instructor is always interested in reactions among those to whom he is giving instruction. The effective administrator is equally conscious of the need to determine his or her subordinates' reactions to what he or she is trying to communicate.
   The principle referred to in the above selection is MOST appropriately called
   A. cognitive dissonance   B. feedback
   C. negative reinforcement   D. noise transmission

9. Of the following, the PRINCIPAL function of an *ombudsman* generally is to
   A. review departmental requests for new data processing equipment so as to reduce duplication
   B. receive and investigate complaints from citizens who are displeased with the actions or non-actions of administrative officials and try to effectuate warranted remedies
   C. review proposed departmental reorganizations in order to advise the chief executive whether or not they are in accordance with the latest principles of proper management structuring
   D. presiding over courts of the judiciary convened to try *sitting* judges

9.____

10. Of the following, the MOST valid reason for recruiting an intermediate-level administrator from outside an agency, rather than from within the agency, normally is to
    A. improve the public image of the agency as a desirable place in which to be employed
    B. reduce the number of potential administrators who must be evaluated prior to filling the position
    C. minimize the morale problems arising from frequent internal staff upgradings
    D. obtain fresh ideas and a fresh viewpoint on agency problems

10.____

11. A MAJOR research finding regarding employee absenteeism is that
    A. absenteeism is likely to be higher on hot days
    B. male employees tend to be absent more than female employees
    C. the way an employee is treated as a definite bearing on absenteeism
    D. the distance employees have to travel is one of the most important factors in absenteeism

11.____

12. Of the following, the supervisory behavior that is of GREATEST benefit to the organization is exhibited by supervisors who
    A. are strict with subordinates about following rules and regulations
    B. encourage subordinates to be interested in the work
    C. are willing to assist with subordinates' work on most occasions
    D. get the most done with available staff and resources

12.____

13. The management of time is one of the critical aspects of any supervisor's performance.
    Therefore, in evaluating a subordinate from the viewpoint of how he manages time, a supervisor should rate HIGHEST the subordinate who
    A. concentrates on each task as he undertakes it
    B. performs at a standard and predictable pace under all circumstances
    C. takes shortened lunch periods when he is busy
    D. tries to do two things simultaneously

14. A MAJOR research finding regarding employee absenteeism is that
    A. absenteeism is likely to be higher on hot days
    B. male employees tend to be absent more than female employees
    C. the way an employee is treated as a definite bearing on absenteeism
    D. the distance employees have to travel is one of the most important factors in absenteeism

15. Of the following, the supervisory behavior that is of GREATEST benefit to the organization is exhibited by supervisors who
    A. are strict with subordinates about following rules and regulations
    B. encourage subordinates to be interested in the work
    C. are willing to assist with subordinates' work on most occasions
    D. get the most done with available staff and resources

16. In order to maintain a proper relationship with a worker who is assigned to staff rather than line functions, a line supervisor should
    A. accept all recommendations of the staff worker
    B. include the staff worker in the conferences called by the supervisor for his subordinates
    C. keep the staff worker informed of developments in the area of his staff assignment
    D. require that the staff worker's recommendations be communicated to the supervisor through the supervisor's own superior

17. Of the following, the GREATEST disadvantage of placing a worker in a staff position under the direct supervision of the supervisor whom he advises is the possibility that the
    A. staff worker will tend to be insubordinate because of a feeling of superiority over the supervisor
    B. staff worker will tend to give advice of the type which the supervisor wants to hear or finds acceptable
    C. supervisor will tend to be mistrustful of the advice of a worker of subordinate rank
    D. supervisor will tend to derive little benefit from the advice because to supervise properly he should know at least as much as his subordinate

18. One factor which might be given consideration in deciding upon the optimum span of control of a supervisor over his immediate subordinates is the position of the supervisor in the hierarchy of the organization.
It is generally considered proper that the number of subordinates immediately supervised by a higher, upper echelon, supervisor
    A. is unrelated to and tends to form no pattern with the number of supervised by lower level supervisors
    B. should be about the same as the number supervised by a lower level supervisor
    C. should be larger than the number supervised by a lower level supervisor
    D. should be smaller than the number supervised by a lower level supervisor

18.____

19. Assume that you are a supervisor and have been assigned to assist the head of a large agency unit. He asks you to prepare a simple, functional organization chart of the unit.
Such a chart would be USEFUL for
    A. favorably impressing members of the public with the important nature of the agency's work
    B. graphically presenting staff relationships which may indicate previously unknown duplications, overlaps, and gaps in job duties
    C. motivating all employees toward better performance because they will have a better understanding of job procedures
    D. subtly and inoffensively making known to the staff in the unit that you are now in a position of responsibility

19.____

20. In some large organizations, management's traditional means of learning about employee dissatisfaction has been in the *open door policy*.
This policy USUALLY means that
    A. management lets it be known that a management representative is generally available to discuss employees' questions, suggestions, and complaints
    B. management sets up an informal employee organization to establish a democratic procedure for orderly representation of employees
    C. employees are encouraged to attempt to resolve dissatisfactions at the lowest possible level of authority
    D. employees are provided with an address or box so that they may safely and anonymously register complaints

20.____

KEY (CORRECT ANSWERS)

1.	B	11.	A
2.	A	12.	D
3.	D	13.	A
4.	B	14.	C
5.	A	15.	D
6.	A	16.	C
7.	B	17.	B
8.	B	18.	D
9.	D	19.	B
10.	C	20.	A

SUPERVISION, ADMINISTRATION, MANAGEMENT AND ORGANIZATION

EXAMINATION SECTION
TEST 1

DIRECTIONS: Each question or incomplete statement is followed by several suggested answers or completions. Select the one that BEST answers the question or completes the statement. *PRINT THE LETTER OF THE CORRECT ANSWER IN THE SPACE AT THE RIGHT.*

1. One of the responsibilities of the supervisor is to provide top administration with information about clients and their problems that will help in the evaluation of existing policies and indicate the need for modifications.
   In order to fulfill this responsibility, it would be MOST essential for the supervisor to

   A. routinely forward all regularly prepared and recurrent reports from his subordinates to his immediate superior
   B. regularly review agency rules, regulations and policies to make sure that he has sufficient knowledge to make appropriate analyses
   C. note repeated instances of failure of staff to correctly administer a policy and schedule staff conferences for corrective training
   D. analyze reports on cases submitted by subordinates, in order to select relevant trend material to be forwarded to his superiors

2. You find that your division has a serious problem because of unusually long delays in filing reports and overdue approvals to private agencies under contract for services.
   The MOST appropriate step to take FIRST in this situation would be to

   A. request additional staff to work on reports and approvals
   B. order staff to work overtime until the backlog is eliminated
   C. impress staff with the importance of expeditious handling of reports and approvals
   D. analyze present procedures for handling reports and approvals

3. When a supervisor finds that he must communicate orally information that is significant enough to affect the entire staff, it would be MOST important to

   A. distribute a written summary of the information to his staff before discussing it orally
   B. tell his subordinate supervisors to discuss this information at individual conferences with their subordinates
   C. call a follow-up meeting of absentees as soon as they return
   D. restate and summarize the information in order to make sure that everyone understands its meaning and implications

4. Of the following, the BEST way for a supervisor to assist a subordinate who has unusually heavy work pressures is to

   A. point out that such pressures go with the job and must be tolerated
   B. suggest to him that the pressures probably result from poor handling of his workload
   C. help him to be selective in deciding on priorities during the period of pressure
   D. ask him to work overtime until the period of pressure is over

5. Leadership is a basic responsibility of the supervisor. The one of the following which would be the LEAST appropriate way to fulfill this role is for the supervisor to

   A. help staff to work up to their capacities in every possible way
   B. encourage independent judgment and actions by staff members
   C. allow staff to participate in decisions within policy limits
   D. take over certain tasks in which he is more competent than his subordinates

6. Assume that you have assigned a very difficult administrative task to one of your best subordinate supervisors, but he is reluctant to take it on because he fears that he will fail in it. It is your judgment, however, that he is quite capable of performing this task.
   The one of the following which is the MOST desirable way for you to handle this situation is to

   A. reassure him that he has enough skill to perform the task and that he will not be penalized if he fails
   B. reassign the task to another supervisor who is more achievement-oriented and more confident of his skills
   C. minimize the importance of the task so that he will feel it is safe for him to attempt it
   D. stress the importance of the task and the dependence of the other staff members on his succeeding in it

7. Assume that a member of your professional staff deliberately misinterprets a new state directive because he fears that its enforcement will have an adverse effect on clients. Although you consider him to be a good supervisor and basically agree with him, you should direct him to comply.
   Of the following, the MOST desirable way for you to handle this situation would be to

   A. avoid a confrontation with him by transferring responsibility for carrying out the directive to another member of your staff
   B. explain to him that you are in a better position than he to assess the implications of the new directive
   C. discuss with him the basic reasons for his misinterpretation and explain why he must comply with the directive
   D. allow him to interpret the directive in his own way as long as he assumes full responsibility for his actions

8. Of the following, the MAIN reason it is important for an administrator in a large organization to properly coordinate the work delegated to subordinates is that such coordination

   A. makes it unnecessary to hold frequent staff meetings and conferences with key staff members
   B. reduces the necessity for regular evaluation of procedures and programs, production and performance of personnel
   C. results in greater economy and stricter accountability for the organization's resources
   D. facilitates integration of the contributions of the numerous staff members who are responsible for specific parts of the total workload

3 (#1)

9. The one of the following which would NOT be an appropriate reason for the formulation of an entirely NEW policy is that it would

   A. serve as a positive affirmation of the agency's function and how it is to be carried out
   B. give focus and direction to the work of the staff, particularly in decision-making
   C. inform the public of the precise conditions under which services will be rendered
   D. provide procedures which constitute uniform methods of carrying out operations

9.____

10. Of the following, it is MOST difficult to formulate policy in an organization where

    A. work assignments are narrowly specialized by units
    B. staff members have varied backgrounds and a wide range of competency
    C. units implementing the same policy are in the same geographic location
    D. staff is experienced and fully trained

10.____

11. For a supervisor to feel that he is responsible for influencing the attitudes of his staff members is GENERALLY considered

    A. *undesirable;* attitudes of adults are emotional factors which usually cannot be changed
    B. *desirable;* certain attitudes can be obstructive and should be modified in order to provide effective service to clients
    C. *undesirable;* the supervisor should be nonjudgmental and accepting of widely different attitudes and social patterns of staff members
    D. *desirable;* influencing attitudes is a teaching responsibility which the supervisor shares with the training specialist

11.____

12. The one of the following which is NOT generally a function of the higher-level supervisor is

    A. projecting the budget and obtaining financial resources
    B. providing conditions conducive to optimum employee production
    C. maintaining records and reports as a basis for accountability and evaluation
    D. evaluating program achievements and personnel effectiveness in accordance with goals and standards

12.____

13. As a supervisor in a recently decentralized services center offering multiple services, you are given responsibility for an orientation program for professional staff on the recent reorganization of the Department.
    Of the following, the MOST appropriate step to take FIRST would be to

    A. organize a series of workshops for subordinate supervisors
    B. arrange a tour of the new geographic area of service
    C. review supervisors' reports, statistical data and other relevant material
    D. develop a resource manual for staff on the reorganized center

13.____

14. Experts generally agree that the content of training sessions should be closely related to workers' practice.
    Of the following, the BEST method of achieving this aim is for the training conference leader to

    A. encourage group discussion of problems that concern staff in their practice
    B. develop closer working relationships with top administration

14.____

C. coordinate with central office to obtain feedback on problems that concern staff
D. observe workers in order to develop a pattern of problems for class discussion

15. The one of the following which is generally the MOST useful teaching tool for professional staff development is

    A. visual aids and tape recordings
    B. professional literature
    C. agency case material
    D. lectures by experts

16. The one of the following which is NOT a good reason for using group conferences as a method of supervision is to

    A. give workers a feeling of mutual support through sharing common problems
    B. save time by eliminating the need for individual conferences
    C. encourage discussion of certain problems that are not as likely to come up in individual conferences
    D. provide an opportunity for developing positive identification with the department and its programs

17. The supervisor, in his role as teacher, applies his teaching in line with his understanding of people and realizes that teaching is a highly individualized process, based on understanding of the worker as a person and as a learner. This statement implies, MOST NEARLY, that the supervisor must help the worker to

    A. overcome his biases
    B. develop his own ways of working
    C. gain confidence in his ability
    D. develop the will to work

18. Of the following, the circumstance under which it would be MOST appropriate to divide a training conference for professional staff into small workshops is when

    A. some of the trainees are not aware of the effect of their attitudes and behavior on others
    B. the trainees need to look at human relations problems from different perspectives
    C. the trainees are faced with several substantially different types of problems in their job assignments
    D. the trainees need to know how to function in many different capacities

19. Of the following, the MAIN reason why it is important to systemically evaluate a specific training program while it is in progress is to

    A. collect data that will serve as a valid basis for improving the agency's overall training program and maintaining control over its components
    B. insure that instruction by training specialists is conducted in a manner consistent with the planned design of the training program
    C. identify areas in which additional or remedial training for the training specialists can be planned and implemented
    D. provide data which are usable in effecting revisions of specific components of the training program

20. Staff development has been defined as an educational process which seeks to provide agency staff with knowledge about specific job responsibilities and to effect changes in staff attitudes and behavior patterns. Assume that you are assigned to define the educational objectives of a specific training program.
In accordance with the above concept, the MOST helpful formulation would be a statement of the

   A. purpose and goals of each training session
   B. generalized patterns of behavior to be developed in the trainees
   C. content material to be presented in the training sessions
   D. kind of behavior to be developed in the trainees and the situations in which this behavior will be applied

21. In teaching personnel under your supervision how to gather and analyze facts before attempting to solve a problem, the one of the following training methods which would be MOST effective is

   A. case study
   B. role playing
   C. programmed learning
   D. planned experience'

22. The importance of analyzing functions traditionally included in the position of caseworker, with a view toward identifying and separating those activities to be performed by the most highly skilled personnel, has been widely discussed.
Of the following, an IMPORTANT *secondary* gain which can result from such differential use of staff is that

   A. supporting job assignments can be given to persons unable to meet the demands of casework, to the satisfaction of all concerned
   B. documentation will be provided on workers who are not suited for all the duties now part of the caseworker's job
   C. caseworkers with a high level of competence in working with people can be rewarded through promotion or merit increases
   D. incompetent workers can be identified and categorized, as a basis for transfer or separation from the service

23. Of the following, a serious DISADVANTAGE of a performance evaluation system based on standardized evaluation factors is that such a system tends to

   A. exacerbate the anxieties of those supervisors who are apprehensive about determining what happens to another person
   B. subject the supervisor to psychological stress by emphasizing the incompatibility of his dual role as both judge and counselor
   C. create organizational conflict by encouraging personnel who wish to enhance their standing to become too aggressive in the performance of their duties
   D. lead many staff members to concentrate on measuring up in terms of the evaluation factors and to disregard other aspects of their work

24. Which of the following would contribute MOST to the achievement of conformity of staff activities and goals to the intent of agency policies and procedures?

   A. Effective communications and organizational discipline
   B. Changing nature of the underlying principles and desired purpose of the policies and procedures

C. Formulation of specific criteria for implementing the policies and procedures
D. Continuous monitoring of the essential effectiveness of agency operations

25. Job enlargement, a management device used by large organizations to counteract the adverse effects of specialization on employee performance, is LEAST likely to improve employee motivation if it is accomplished by

    A. lengthening the job cycle and adding a large number of similar tasks
    B. allowing the employee to use a greater variety of skills
    C. increasing the scope and complexity of the employee's job
    D. giving the employee more opportunities to make decisions

25. _____

KEY (CORRECT ANSWERS)

1.	D	11.	B
2.	D	12.	A
3.	D	13.	A
4.	C	14.	A
5.	D	15.	C
6.	A	16.	B
7.	C	17.	B
8.	D	18.	C
9.	D	19.	A
10.	B	20.	D

21.	A
22.	A
23.	D
24.	A
25.	A

TEST 2

DIRECTIONS: Each question or incomplete statement is followed by several suggested answers or completions. Select the one that BEST answers the question or completes the statement. *PRINT THE LETTER OF THE CORRECT ANSWER IN THE SPACE AT THE RIGHT.*

1. When a supervisor requires approval for case action on a higher level, the process used is known as

    A. administrative clearance
    B. going outside channels
    C. administrative consultation
    D. delegation of authority

2. In delegating authority to his subordinates, the one of the following to which a GOOD supervisor should give PRIMARY consideration is the

    A. results expected of them
    B. amount of power to be delegated
    C. amount of responsibility to be delegated
    D. their skill in the performance of present tasks

3. Of the following, the type of decision which could be SAFELY delegated to LOWER-LEVEL staff without undermining basic supervisory responsibility is one which

    A. involves a commitment that can be fulfilled only over a long period of time
    B. has fairly uncertain goals and premises
    C. has the possibility of modification built into it
    D. may generate considerable resistance from those affected by it

4. Of the following, the MOST valuable contribution made by the informal organization in a large public service agency is that such an organization

    A. has goals and values which are usually consistent with and reinforce those of the formal organization
    B. is more flexible than the formal organization and more adaptable to changing conditions
    C. has a communications system which often contributes to the efficiency of the formal organization
    D. represents a sound basis on which to build the formal organizational structure

5. Of the following, the condition under which it would be MOST useful for an agency to develop detailed procedures is when

    A. subordinate supervisory personnel need a structure to help them develop greater independence
    B. employees have little experience or knowledge of how to perform certain assigned tasks
    C. coordination of agency activities is largely dependent upon personal contact
    D. agency activities must continually adjust to changes in local circumstances

6. Assume that a certain administrator has the management philosophy that his agency's responsibility is to routinize existing operations, meet each day's problems as they arise, and resolve problems with a minimum of residual effect upon himself or his agency. The possibility that this official would be able to administer his agency without running into serious difficulties would be MORE likely during a period of

    A. economic change
    B. social change
    C. economic crisis
    D. social and economic stability

7. Some large organizations have adopted the practice of allowing each employee to establish his own performance goals, and then later evaluate himself in an individual conference with his immediate supervisor.
   Of the following, a DRAWBACK of this approach is that the employee

   A. may set his goals too low and rate himself too highly
   B. cannot control those variables which may improve his performance
   C. has no guidelines for improving his performance
   D. usually finds it more difficult to criticize himself than to accept criticism from others

8. Decentralization of services cannot completely eliminate the requirement of central office approval for certain case actions. The MOST valid reason for complaint about this requirement is that

   A. unavoidable delay created by referral to central office may cause serious problems for the client
   B. it may lower morale of supervisors who are not given the authority to take final action on urgent cases
   C. the concept of role responsibility is minimized
   D. the objective of delegated responsibility tends to be negated

9. Which of the following would be the MOST useful administrative tool for the purpose of showing the sequence of operations and staff involved? A(n)

   A. organization chart
   B. flow chart
   C. manual of operating procedures
   D. statistical review

10. The prevailing pattern of organization in large public agencies consists of a limited span of control and organization by function or, at lower levels, process.
    Of the following, the PRINCIPAL effect which this pattern of organization has on the management of work is that it

    A. reduces the management burden in significant ways
    B. creates a time lag between the perception of a problem and action on it
    C. makes it difficult to direct and observe employee performance
    D. facilitates the development of employees with managerial ability

11. The one of the following which would be the MOST appropriate way to reduce tensions between line and staff personnel in public service agencies is to

    A. provide in-service training that will increase the sensitivity of line and staff personnel to their respective roles
    B. assign to staff personnel the role of providing assistance only when requested by line personnel
    C. separate staff from line personnel and provide staff with its own independent reward structure
    D. give line and staff personnel equal status in making decisions

12. In determining the appropriate span of control for subordinate supervisors, which of the following principles should be followed? The more

    A. complex the work, the broader the effective span of control
    B. similar the jobs being supervised, the more narrow the effective span of control

C. interdependent the jobs being supervised, the more narrow the effective span of control
D. unpredictable the work, the broader the effective span of control

13. A method sometimes used in public service agencies to improve upward communication is to require subordinate supervisory staff to submit to top management monthly narrative reports of any problems which they deem important for consideration.
Of the following, a major DISADVANTAGE of this method is that it may

13.____

A. enable subordinate supervisors to avoid thinking about their problems by simply referring such matters to their superiors
B. obscure important issues so that they are not given appropriate attention
C. create a need for numerous staff conferences in order to handle all of the reported problems
D. encourage some subordinate supervisors to focus on irrelevant matters and compete with each other in the length and content of their reports

14. The use of a committee as an approach to the problem of coordinating interdepartmental activities can present difficulties if the committee functions PRIMARILY as a(n)

14.____

A. means of achieving personal objectives and goals
B. instrument for coordinating activities that flow across departmental lines
C. device for involving subordinate personnel in the decision-making process
D. means of giving representation to competing interest groups

15. A study was recently made of the attitudes and perceptions of a sample of workers who had experienced a major organizational change and redefinition of their jobs as a result of separation of certain functions.
Questionnaires administered to these workers indicated that a disproportionate number of workers in the larger agencies were dissatisfied with the reorganization and their new assignments.
Of the following, the MOST plausible reason for this dissatisfaction is that workers in larger agencies are

15.____

A. less likely to be known to management and to be personally disciplined if they expressed dissatisfaction with their new roles
B. less likely to have the opportunity to participate in planning a reorganization and to be given consideration for the assignments they preferred
C. given a shorter lead period to implement the changes and therefore had insufficient time to plan the reorganization and carry it out efficiently
D. usually made up of more older members who have had routinized their work according to habit and find it more difficult to adjust to change

16. An article which recently appeared in a professional journal presents a proposal for participatory leadership, in which the goal of supervision would be development of subordinates' self-reliance, with the premise that each staff member is held accountable for his own performance.
The one of the following which would NOT be a desirable outcome of this type of supervision is the

16.____

A. necessity for subordinates to critically examine their performance
B. development by some subordinates of skills not possessed by the supervisor

C. establishment of a quality control unit for sample checking and identification of errors
D. relaxation of demands made on the supervisor

17. The "management by objectives" concept is a major development in the administration of services organizations. The purpose of this approach is to establish a system for

    A. reduction of waiting time
    B. planning and controlling work output
    C. consolidation of organizational units
    D. work measurement

18. Assume that you encounter a serious administrative problem in implementing a new program. After consulting with the members of your staff individually, you come up with several alternate solutions.
Of the following, the procedure which would be MOST appropriate for evaluating the relative merits of each solution would be to

    A. try all of them on a limited experimental basis
    B. break the problem down into its component parts and analyze the effect of each solution on each component in terms of costs and benefits
    C. break the problem down into its component parts, eliminate all intangibles, and measure the effect of the tangible aspects of each solution on each component in terms of costs and benefits
    D. bring the matter before your weekly staff conference, discuss the relative merits of each alternate solution, and then choose the one favored by the majority of the conference

19. When establishing planning objectives for a service program under your supervision, the one of the following principles which should be followed is that objectives

    A. are rarely verifiable if they are qualitative
    B. should be few in number and of equal importance
    C. should cover as many of the activities of the program as possible
    D. should be set in the light of assumptions about future funding

20. Assume that you have been assigned responsibility for coordinating various aspects of a program in a community services center. Which of the following administrative concepts would NOT be applicable to this assignment?

    A. Functional job analysis
    B. Peer group supervision
    C. Differential use of staff
    D. Systems design

21. Good administrative practice includes the use of outside consultants as an effective technique in achieving agency objectives. However, the one of the following which would NOT be an appropriate role for the consultant is

    A. provision of technical or professional expertise not otherwise available in the agency
    B. administrative direction of a new program activity
    C. facilitating coordination and communication among agency staff
    D. objective measurement of the effectiveness of agency services

22. Of the following, the MOST common fault of research projects attempting to measure the effectiveness of social programs has been their

    A. questionable methodology
    B. inaccurate findings
    C. unrealistic expectations
    D. lack of objectivity

22._____

23. One of the most difficult tasks of supervision in a modern public agency is teaching workers to cope with the hostile reactions of clients. In order to help the disconcerted worker analyze and understand a client's hostile behavior, the supervisor should FIRST

    A. encourage the worker to identify with the client's frustrations and deprivations
    B. give the worker a chance to express and accept his feelings about the client
    C. ask the worker to review his knowledge of the client and his circumstances
    D. explain to the worker that the client's anger is not directed at the worker personally

23._____

24. Determination of the level of participation, or how much of the public should participate in a given project, is a vital step in community organization.
In order to make this determination, the FIRST action that should be taken is to

    A. develop the participants
    B. fix the goals of the project
    C. evaluate community interest in the project
    D. enlist the cooperation of community leaders

24._____

25. The one of the following which would be the MOST critical factor for SUCCESSFUL operation of a decentralized system of programs and services is

    A. periodic review and evaluation of services delivered at the community level
    B. transfer of decision-making authority to the community level wherever feasible
    C. participation of indigenous non-professionals in service delivery
    D. formulation of quantitative plans for dealing with community problems wherever feasible

25._____

KEY (CORRECT ANSWERS)

1. A
2. A
3. C
4. C
5. B

6. D
7. A
8. A
9. B
10. B

11. A
12. C
13. D
14. A
15. B

16. D
17. B
18. C
19. D
20. B

21. B
22. C
23. B
24. B
25. B

TEST 3

DIRECTIONS: Each question or incomplete statement is followed by several suggested answers or completions. Select the one that BEST answers the question or completes the statement. *PRINT THE LETTER OF THE CORRECT ANSWER IN THE SPACE AT THE RIGHT.*

1. Douglas McGregor's theory of human motivation classifies worker behavior into two distinct categories: Theory X and Theory Y. Theory X, the traditional view, states that the average man dislikes to work and will avoid work if he can, unless coerced. Theory Y holds essentially the opposite view. The executive can apply both of these theories to worker behavior BEST if he

    A. follows an "open-door" policy only with respect to his immediate subordinates
    B. recognizes his subordinates' mental and social needs as well as agency needs
    C. recognizes that executive responsibility is primarily limited to fulfillment of agency productivity goals
    D. directs his subordinate managers to follow a policy of close supervision

1.____

2. In interpersonal communications it is of paramount importance to determine whether or not what has been said has been understood by others. One of the MOST important sources of such information is known as

    A. the halo effect   B. evaluation
    C. feedback   D. quantitative analysis

2.____

3. The grapevine most often provides a USEFUL service by

    A. correcting some of the deficiencies of the formal communication system
    B. rapidly conveying a true picture of events
    C. involving staff in current organizational changes
    D. interfering with the operation of the formal communication system

3.____

4. People who are in favor of a leadership style in which the subordinates help make decisions, contend that it produces favorable effects in a work unit. According to these people, which of the following is NOT likely to be an effect of such "participative management"?

    A. Reduced turnover
    B. Accelerated learning of duties
    C. Greater acceptance of change
    D. Reduced acceptance of the work unit's goals

4.____

5. Employees of a public service agency will be MOST likely to develop meaningful goals for both the agency and the employee and become committed to attaining them if supervisors

    A. allow them unilaterally to set their own goals
    B. provide them with a clear understanding of the premises underlying the agency's goals
    C. encourage them to concentrate on setting only short-range goals for themselves
    D. periodically review the agency's goals in order to suggest changes in accordance with current conditions

5.____

6. The insights of Chester Barnard have influenced the development of management thought in significant ways. He is MOST closely identified with a position that has become known as the

   A. acceptance theory of authority
   B. principle of the manager's or executive's span of control
   C. "Theory X" and "Theory Y" dichotomy
   D. unity of command principle

7. If a manager believes that man is primarily motivated by economic incentives and, above all, seeks security, he MOST usually should operate on the assumption that his subordinates

   A. need to be closely directed and have relatively little ambition
   B. are more responsive to the social forces of their peer group than to the incentives of management
   C. are capable of learning not only to accept but to seek responsibility
   D. are capable of responding favorably to many different kinds of managerial strategies

8. Of the following, the MOST important reason why it is in the interest of public service agencies to involve subordinate personnel in setting goals is that the more committed employees are to the goals of their agency the

   A. *more* likely they are to develop a desire for the agency's achievement of success
   B. *more* likely they are to prefer difficult rather than easy tasks
   C. *more* likely they are to perceive their individual performance as a reliable indicator of the agency's performance
   D. *less* likely they are to choose unreasonably difficult goals

9. As a result of gaining more recent knowledge about motivation, modern executives have had to rethink their notions about what motivates their subordinate managers. Which of the following factors is GENERALLY considered MOST important in modern motivation theory?

   A. Fringe benefits
   B. Working conditions
   C. Recognition of good work performance
   D. Education and experience required for the job

10. Of the following, the MAIN reason why cooperative interrelationships among personnel are more likely than competitive interrelationships to promote efficiency in the operation of a public service agency is that cooperation

    A. allows for a greater degree of specialization by function
    B. increases the opportunities for employees to check on each others' work
    C. provides a feeling of identification with the organization and enhances the desire for accomplishment
    D. improves the capacity of employees to acquire knowledge and learn new skills

11. Four statements are given below. Three of them describe approaches which are desirable in developing a program of employee motivation. The one which does NOT describe such an approach is:

   A. "Establish attainable goals to give employees a sense of achievement."
   B. "Largely discount the self-interest motive because it is impractical to consider it."
   C. "Allow for the participation of persons included in the plans."
   D. "Base plans on group considerations as well as individual considerations."

12. It is GENERALLY acknowledged that certain conditions should exist to insure that a subordinate will decide to accept a communication as being authoritative. Which of the following is LEAST valid as a condition which should exist?

   A. The subordinate understands the communication
   B. At the time of the subordinate's decision, he views the communication as consistent with the organization's purpose and his personal interest
   C. At the time of the subordinate's decision, he views the communication as more consistent with his personal purpose than with the organization's interests
   D. The subordinate is mentally and physically able to comply with the communication

13. In exploring the effects that employee participation has on putting changes in work methods into effect, certain relationships have been established between participation and productivity. It has MOST generally been found that HIGHEST productivity occurs in groups that are given

   A. participation in the process of change only through representatives of their group
   B. no participation in the change process
   C. full participation in the change process
   D. intermittent participation in the process of change

14. Of the following statements, the one which represents a trend LEAST likely to occur in the area of employee-management relations is that:

   A. Employees will exert more influence on decisions affecting their interests.
   B. Technological change will have a stronger impact on organizations' human resources.
   C. Labor will judge management according to company profits.
   D. Government will play a larger role in balancing the interests of the parties in labor-management affairs.

15. Members of an organization must satisfy several fundamental psychological needs in order to be happy and productive. The broadest and MOST basic needs are

   A. achievement, recognition and acceptance
   B. competition, recognition and accomplishment
   C. salary increments and recognition
   D. acceptance of competition and economic reward

16. Morale has been defined as the capacity of a group of people to pull together steadily for a common purpose. Morale thus defined is MOST generally dependent on which one of the following conditions?

   A. Job security
   B. Group and individual self-confidence
   C. Organizational efficiency
   D. Physical health of the individuals

4 (#3)

17. Assume that consideration is being given to forming a committee for the purpose of getting a new program under way which requires the coordination of several organizational units. Which one of the following would be a MAJOR weakness of using the "committee" approach in this situation?

    A. Its inappropriateness for decision-making
    B. The necessity to include line and staff employees
    C. The difficulty of achieving proper representation
    D. Its independence from the formal organization

18. Which of the following techniques is NOT used as an approach to encourage communication between individuals at the same level?

    A. The informal organization
    B. The chain of command
    C. Committee meetings
    D. Distribution of written reports

19. In everyday actual operations, downward communications MOST often concern

    A. specific directives about job performance
    B. information about worker performance
    C. information about the rationale of the job
    D. information to indoctrinate the organization's staff on goals to be achieved

20. Communication has been thought of for a long time as a vital process in a formal organization system. Of the following, the MOST accurate statement that can be made concerning this process is that

    A. decision-making depends on communication and organizational structure
    B. communication does not interact but is interdependent with organizational structure and decision-making
    C. effective decision-making is dependent on organizational structure but not on communication
    D. communication is dependent on the decision-making process but not on organizational structure

21. In coaching a subordinate manager in the use of the type of management in which subordinate employees participate, an executive would be MOST accurate in emphasizing that participative management

    A. uses consultative as opposed to democratic techniques
    B. uses democratic as opposed to consultative techniques
    C. requires the involvement of subordinates while reserving for the superior the right to make decisions
    D. requires involving subordinates and giving them the right to make most decisions

22. In most work situations, employees tend to form informal groups and relationships. The BEST way for a supervisor interested in high productivity to deal with such groups and relationships is to

    A. take them into account as much as possible when making work assignments and schedules
    B. ignore them, since such relationships and groups usually have no effect on work productivity

C. attempt to destroy such groups and relationships since they are usually counter-productive
D. ignore them, even though they are usually counterproductive, since nothing can be done about them

23. Assume that in an office an entirely new method has been introduced in the handling of applications for service and related information. Employees USUALLY approach such a sudden change in their work routine with an attitude of

    A. *apprehension,* chiefly because such a change makes them uncertain of their position
    B. *indifference,* chiefly because most people don't care what they are doing, as long as they are paid
    C. *approval,* chiefly because such a change provides a welcome change of pace in their work
    D. *acceptance,* mainly because most people prefer changes to the same routines

23.____

24. In what order should the following steps be taken when revising office procedure?
    I. To develop the improved method as determined by time and motion studies and effective workplace layout
    II. To find out how the task is now performed
    III. To apply the new method
    IV. To analyze the current method

    The CORRECT order is:

    A. IV, II, I, III   B. II, I, III, IV
    C. I, II, IV, III   D. II, IV, I, III

24.____

25. In contrast to broad spans of control, narrow spans of control are MOST likely to

    A. provide opportunity for more personal contact between superior and subordinate
    B. encourage decentralization
    C. stress individual initiative
    D. foster group or team effort

25.____

KEY (CORRECT ANSWERS)

1. B
2. C
3. A
4. D
5. B

6. A
7. A
8. A
9. C
10. C

11. B
12. C
13. C
14. C
15. A

16. B
17. A
18. B
19. A
20. A

21. C
22. A
23. A
24. D
25. A

SUPERVISION, ADMINISTRATION, MANAGEMENT, AND ORGANIZATION

EXAMINATION SECTION

TEST 1

DIRECTIONS: Each question or incomplete statement is followed by several suggested answers or completions. Select the one that BEST answers the question or completes the statement. *PRINT THE LETTER OF THE CORRECT ANSWER IN THE SPACE AT THE RIGHT.*

1. In coaching a subordinate on the nature of decision-making, an executive would be right if he stated that the one of the following which is general the BEST definition of decision-making is:
   A. Choosing between alternatives
   B. Making diagnoses of feasible ends
   C. Making diagnoses of feasible means
   D. Comparing alternatives

2. Of the following, which one would be LEAST valid as a purpose of an organizational policy statement?
   To
   A. keep personnel from performing improper actions and functions on routine matters
   B. prevent the mishandling of non-routine matters
   C. provide management personnel with a tool that precludes the need for their use of judgment
   D. provide standard decisions and approaches in handling problems of a recurrent nature

3. Much has been written criticizing bureaucratic organizations. Current thinking on the subject is GENERALLY that
   A. bureaucracy is on the way out
   B. bureaucracy, though not perfect, is unlikely to be replaced
   C. bureaucratic organizations are most effective in dealing with constant change
   D. bureaucratic organizations are most effective when dealing with sophisticated customers or clients

4. The development of alternate plans as a major step in planning will normally result in the planner having several possible courses of action available. GENERALLY, this is
   A. *desirable*, since such development helps to determine the most suitable alternative and to provide for the unexpected
   B. *desirable*, since such development makes the use of planning premises and constraints unnecessary

C. *undesirable*, since the planners should formulate only one way of achieving given goals at a given time
D. *undesirable*, since such action restricts efforts to modify the planning to take advantage of opportunities

5. The technique of departmentation by task force includes the assigning of a team or task force to a definite project or block of work which extends from the beginning to the completing of a wanted and definite type and quantity of work. Of the following, the MOST important actor aiding the successful use of this technique *normally* is
    A. having the task force relatively large, at least one hundred members
    B. having a definite project termination date established
    C. telling each task force member what his next assignment will be only after the current project ends
    D. utilizing it only for projects that are regularly recurring

6. With respect to communication in small group settings such as may occur in business, government, and the military, it is generally TRUE that people usually derive more satisfaction and are usually more productive under conditions which
    A. permit communication only with superiors
    B. permit the minimum intragroup communication possible
    C. are generally restricted by management
    D. allow open communication among all group members

7. If an executive were asked to list some outstanding features of decentralization, which one of the following would NOT be such a feature?
Decentralization
    A. provides decision-making experience for lower level managers
    B. promotes uniformity of policy
    C. is a relatively new concept in management
    D. is similar to the belief in encouragement of free enterprise

8. Modern management experts have emphasized the importance of the informal organization in motivating employees to increase productivity.
Of the following, the characteristic which would have the MOST direct influence on employee motivation is the tendency of members of the informal organization to
    A. resist change
    B. establish their own norms
    C. have similar outside interests
    D. set substantially higher goals than those of management

9. According to leading management experts, the decision-making process contains separate and distinct steps that must be taken in an orderly sequence.
Of the following arrangements, which one is in CORRECT order?

A. I. Search for alternatives; II. diagnosis; III. comparison; IV. choice
B. I. Diagnose; II. comparison; III. search for alternatives; IV. choice
C. I. Diagnose; II. search for alternatives; III. comparison; IV. choice
D. I. Diagnose; II. search for alternatives; III. choice; IV. comparison

10. Of the following, the growth of professionalism in large organizations can PRIMARILY be expected to result in 10.____
    A. greater equalization of power
    B. increased authoritarianism
    C. greater organizational disloyalty
    D. increased promotion opportunities

11. Assume an executive carries out his responsibilities to his staff according to what is now known about managerial leadership. 11.____
    Which of the following statements would MOST accurately reflect his assumptions about proper management?
    A. Efficiency in operations results from allowing the human element to participate in a minimal way.
    B. Efficient operation result from balancing work considerations with personnel considerations.
    C. Efficient operation results from a workforce committed to its self-interest.
    D. Efficient operation results from staff relationships that produce a friendly work climate.

12. Assume that an executive is called upon to conduct a management audit. To do this properly, he would have to take certain steps in a specific sequence. 12.____
    Of the following steps, which step should this manager take FIRST?
    A. Managerial performance must be surveyed.
    B. A method of reporting must be established.
    C. Management auditing procedures and documentation must be developed.
    D. Criteria for the audit must be considered.

13. If a manager is required to conduct a scientific investigation of an organizational problem, the FIRST step he should take is to 13.____
    A. state his assumptions about the problem
    B. carry out a search for background information
    C. choose the right approach to investigate the validity of his assumptions
    D. define and state the problem

14. An executive would be right to assert that the principle of delegation states that decisions should be made PRIMARILY 14.____
    A. by persons in an executive capacity qualified to make them
    B. by persons in a non-executive capacity
    C. at as low an organization level of authority as practicable
    D. by the next lower level of authority

15. Of the following, which one is NOT regarded by management authorities as a FUNDAMENTAL characteristic of an *ideal* bureaucracy?
    A. Division of labor and specialization
    B. An established hierarchy
    C. Decentralization of authority
    D. A set of operating rules and regulations

16. As the number of subordinates in a manager's span of control increases, the ACTUAL number of possible relationships
    A. increases disproportionately to the number of subordinates
    B. increases in equal number to the number of subordinates
    C. reaches a stable level
    D. will first increase then slowly decrease

17. An executive's approach to controlling the activities of his subordinates concentrated on ends rather than means, and was diagnostic rather than punitive.
    This manager may MOST properly be characterized as using the managerial technique of management-by-
    A. exception   B. objectives   C. crisis   D. default

18. In conducting a training session on the administrative control process, which of the following statements would be LEAST valid for an executive to make?
    Controlling
    A. requires checking upon assignments to see what is being done
    B. involves comparing what is being done to what ought to be done
    C. requires corrective action when what is being done does not meet expectations
    D. occurs after all the other managerial processes have been performed

19. The "brainstorming" technique for creative solutions of management problems MOST generally consists of
    A. bringing staff together in an exchange of a quantity of freewheeling ideas
    B. isolating individual staff members to encourage thought
    C. developing improved office procedures
    D. preparation of written reports on complex problems

20. Computer systems hardware MOST often operates in relation to which one of the following steps in solving a data-processing problem?
    A. Determining the problem
    B. Defining and stating the problem
    C. Implementing the programmed solution
    D. Completing the documentation of every unexplored solution

21. There is a tendency in management to upgrade objectives.
    This trend is generally regarded as
    A. *desirable*; the urge to improve is demonstrated by adopting objectives that have been adjusted to provide improved service

B. *undesirable*; the typical manager searches for problems which obstruct his objectives
C. *desirable*; it is common for a manager to find that the details of an immediate operation have occupied so much of his time that he has lost sight of the basic overall objective
D. *undesirable*; efforts are wasted when they are expended on a mass of uncertain objectives, since the primary need of most organizations is a single target or several major ones

22. Of the following, it is generally LEAST effective for an executive to delegate authority where working conditions involve
    A. rules establishing normal operating procedures
    B. consistent methods of operation
    C. rapidly changing work standards
    D. complex technology

22.____

23. If an executive was explaining the difficulty of making decisions under *risk* conditions, he would be MOST accurate if he said that such decisions would be difficult to make when the decision maker has _____ information and experience and can expect _____ outcomes for each action.
    A. limited; many
    B. much; many
    C. much; few
    D. limited; few

23.____

24. If an executive were asked to list some outstanding features of centralized organization, which one of the following would be INCORRECT?
    Centralized organization
    A. lessens risks of errors by unskilled subordinates
    B. utilizes the skills of specialized experts at a central location
    C. produces uniformity of policy and non-uniformity of action
    D. enables closer control of operations than a decentralized set-up

24.____

25. It is possible for an organization's management to test whether or not the organization has a sound structure.
    Of the following, which one is NOT a test of soundness in an organization's structure?
    The
    A. ability to replace key personnel with minimum loss of effectiveness
    B. ability of information and decisions to flow more freely through the *grapevine* than through formal channels
    C. provision for orderly organizational growth with the ability to handle change as the need arises.

25.____

KEY (CORRECT ANSWERS)

1.	A	11.	B
2.	C	12.	D
3.	B	13.	D
4.	A	14.	C
5.	B	15.	C
6.	D	16.	A
7.	B	17.	B
8.	B	18.	D
9.	C	19.	A
10.	A	20.	C

21. A
22. C
23. A
24. C
25. B

TEST 2

DIRECTIONS: Each question or incomplete statement is followed by several suggested answers or completions. Select the one that BEST answers the question or completes the statement. *PRINT THE LETTER OF THE CORRECT ANSWER IN THE SPACE AT THE RIGHT.*

1. Management experts generally believe that computer-based management information systems (MIS) have greater potential for improving the process of management than any other development in recent decades.
   The one of the following which MOST accurately describes the objectives of MIS is to
   A. provide information for decision-making on planning, initiating, and controlling the operations of the various units of the organization
   B. establish mechanization of routine functions such as clerical records, payroll, inventory, and accounts receivable in order to promote economy and efficiency
   C. computerize decision-making on planning, initiative, organizing, and controlling the operations of an organization
   D. provide accurate facts and figures on the various programs of the organization to be used for purposes of planning and research

2. The one of the following which is the BEST application on the *management-by-exception* principle is that this principle
   A. stimulates communication and aids in management of crisis situations, thus reducing the frequency of decision-making
   B. saves time and reserves top-management decisions only for crisis situations, thus reducing the frequency of decision-making
   C. stimulates communication, saves time, and reduces the frequency of decision-making
   D. is limited to crisis-management situations

3. It is generally recognized that each organization is dependent upon availability of qualified personnel.
   Of the following, the MOST important factor affecting the availability of qualified people to each organization is
   A. innovations in technology and science
   B. the general decline in the educational levels of our population
   C. the rise of sentiment against racial discrimination
   D. pressure by organized community groups

4. A fundamental responsibility of all managers is to decide what physical facilities and equipment are needed to help attain basic goals.
   Good planning for the purchase and use of equipment is seldom easy to do and is complicated MOST by the fact that
   A. organizations rarely have stable sources of supply
   B. nearly all managers tend to be better at personnel planning than at equipment planning

C. decisions concerning physical resources are made too often on a *crash basis* rather than under carefully prepared policies
D. legal rulings relative to depreciation fluctuate very frequently

5. In attempting to reconcile managerial objectives and an individual employee's goals, it is generally LEAST desirable for management to
   A. recognize the capacity of the individual to contribute toward realization of managerial goals
   B. encourage self-development of the employee to exceed minimum job performance
   C. consider an individual employee's work separately from other employees
   D. demonstrate that an employee advances only to the extent that he contributes directly to the accomplishment of stated goals

6. As a management tool for discovering individual training needs a job analysis would generally be of LEAST assistance in determining
   A. the performance requirements of individual jobs
   B. actual employee performance on the job
   C. acceptable standards of performance
   D. training needs for individual jobs

7. One of the major concerns of organizational managers today is how the spread of automation will affect them and the status of their positions. Realistically speaking, one can say that the MOST likely effect of our newer forms of highly automated technology on managers will be to
   A. make most top-level positions superfluous or obsolete
   B. reduce the importance of managerial work in general
   C. replace the work of managers with the work of technicians
   D. increase the importance of and demand for top managerial personnel

8. Which one of the following is LEAST likely to be an area or cause of trouble in the use of staff people (e.g., assistants to the administrator)?
   A. Misunderstanding of the role the staff people are supposed to play, as a result of vagueness of definition of their duties and authority
   B. Tendency of staff personnel almost always to be older than line personnel at comparable salary levels with who they must deal
   C. Selection of staff personnel who fail to have simultaneously both competence in their specialties and skill in staff work
   D. The staff person fails to understand mixed staff and operating duties

9. The one of the following which is the BEST measure of decentralization in an agency is the
   A. amount of checking required on decisions made at lower levels in the chain of command
   B. amount of checking required on decisions made at lower levels of the chain of command and the number of functions affected thereby
   C. number of functions affected by decisions made at higher levels
   D. number of functions affected by middle echelon decision-making

10. Which of the following is generally NOT a valid statement with respect to the supervisory process?
    A. General supervision is more effective than close supervision.
    B. Employee-centered supervisors lead more effectively than do production-centered supervisors.
    C. Employee satisfaction is directly related to productivity.
    D. Low-producing supervisors use techniques that are different from high-producing supervisors.

10._____

11. The one of the following which is the MOST essential element for proper evaluation of the performance of subordinate supervisors is a
    A. careful definition of each supervisor's specific job responsibilities and of his progress in meeting mutually agreed upon work goals
    B. system of rewards and penalties based on each supervisor's progress in meeting clearly defined performance standards
    C. definition of personality traits, such as industry, initiative, dependability, and cooperativeness, required for effective job performance
    D. breakdown of each supervisor's job into separate components and a rating of his performance on each individual task

11._____

12. The one of the following which is the PRINCIPAL advantage of specialization for the operating efficiency of a public service agency is that specialization
    A. reduces the amount of red tape in coordinating the activities of mutually dependent departments
    B. simplifies the problem of developing adequate job controls
    C. provides employees with a clear understanding of the relationship of their activities to the overall objectives of the agency
    D. reduces destructive competition for power between departments

12._____

13. Of the following, the group which generally benefits MOST from supervisory training programs in public service agencies are those supervisors who have
    A. accumulated a long period of total service to the agency
    B. responsibility for a large number of subordinate personnel
    C. been in the supervisory ranks for a long period of time
    D. a high level of formalized academic training

13._____

14. A list of conditions which encourages good morale inside a work group would NOT include a
    A. high rate of agreement among group members on values and objectives
    B. tight control system to minimize the risk of individual error
    C. good possibility that joint action will accomplish goals
    D. past history of successful group accomplishment

14._____

15. Of the following, the MOST important factor to be considered in selecting a training strategy or program is the
    A. requirements of the job to be performed by the trainees
    B. educational level or prior training of the trainees
    C. size of the training group
    D. quality and competence of available training specialists

15._____

16. Of the following, the one which is considered to be LEAST characteristic of the higher ranks of management is
    A. that higher levels of management benefit from modern technology
    B. that success is measured by the extent to which objectives are achieved
    C. the number of subordinates that directly report to an executive
    D. the de-emphasis of individual and specialized performance

17. Assume that an executive is preparing a training syllabus to be used in training members of his staff.
    Which of the following would NOT be a valid principle of the learning process for this manager to keep in mind in the preparation of the training syllabus?
    A. When a person has thoroughly learned a task, it takes a lot of effort to create a little more improvement.
    B. In complicated learning situations, there is a period in which an additional period of practice produces an equal amount of improvement in learning.
    C. The less a person knows about the task, the slower the initial progress.
    D. The more the person knows about the risk, the slower the initial progress.

18. Of the following, which statement BEST illustrates when collective bargaining agreements are working well?
    A. Executives strongly support subordinate managers.
    B. The management rights clause in the contract is clear and enforced.
    C. Contract provisions are competently interpreted.
    D. The provisions of the agreement are properly interpreted, communicated, and observed.

19. An executive who wishes to encourage subordinates to communicate freely with him about a job-related problem should FIRST
    A. state his own position on the problem before listening to the subordinates' ideas
    B. invite subordinates to give their own opinions on the problem
    C. ask subordinates for their reactions to his own ideas about the problem
    D. guard the confidentiality of management information about the problem

20. The ability to deal constructively with intra-organizational conflict is an essential attribute of the successful manager.
    The one of the following types of conflict which would be LEAST difficult to handle constructively is a situation in which there is
    A. agreement on objectives, but disagreement as to the probable results of adopting the various alternatives
    B. agreement on objectives, disagreement on alternative courses of action, and relative certainty as to the outcome of one of the alternatives
    C. disagreement on objectives and on alternate courses of action, but relative certainty as to the outcome of the alternatives
    D. disagreement on objectives and on alternative course of action, but uncertainty as to the outcome of the alternatives

21. Which of the following statements is LEAST accurate in describing formal job evaluation and wage and salary classification plans?
    A. Parties that disagree on wage matters can examine an established system rather than unsupported opinions.
    B. The use of such plans tends to overlook the effect of age and seniority of employees on job values in the plan.
    C. Such plans can eliminate salary controversies in organizations designing and using them properly.
    D. These plans are not particularly useful in checking on executive compensation.

22. In carrying out disciplinary action, the MOST important procedure for all managers to follow is to
    A. sell all levels of management on the need for discipline from the organization's viewpoint
    B. follow up on a disciplinary action and not assume that the action has been effective
    C. convince all executives that proper discipline is a legitimate tool for their use
    D. convince all executives that they need to display confidence in the organization's rules

Questions 23-25.

DIRECTIONS: Questions 23 through 25 are to be answered on the basis of the following situation. Richard Ford, a top administrator, is responsible for output in his organization. Because productivity had been lagging for two periods in a row, Ford decided to establish a committee of his subordinate managers to investigate the reasons for the poor performance and to make recommendations for improvements. After two meetings, the committee came to the conclusions and made the recommendations that follow:

Output forecasts had been handed down from the top without prior consultation with middle management and first level supervision. Lines of authority and responsibility had been unclear. The planning and control process should be decentralized.
After receiving the committee's recommendations, Ford proceeded to take the following actions:
Ford decided he would retain final authority to establish quotas but would delegate to the middle managers the responsibility for meeting quotas.
After receiving Ford's decision, the middle managers proceeded to delegate to the first-line supervisors the authority to establish their own quotas. The middle managers eventually received and combined the first-line supervisors' quotas so that these conformed with Ford's.

23. Ford's decision to delegate responsibility for meeting quotas to the middle managers is INCONSISTENT with sound management principles because of which one of the following?
    A. Ford shouldn't have involved himself in the first place.
    B. Middle managers do not have the necessary skills.

C. Quotas should be established by the chief executive.
D. Responsibility should not be delegated.

24. The principle of co-extensiveness of responsibility and authority bears on Ford's decision.
In this case, it IMPLIES that
    A. authority should exceed responsibility
    B. authority should be delegated to match the degree of responsibility
    C. both authority and responsibility should be retained and not delegated
    D. responsibility should be delegated but authority should be retained

25. The middle manager's decision to delegate to the first-line supervisors the authority to establish quotas was INCORRECTLY reasoned because
    A. delegation and control must go together
    B. first-line supervisors are in no position to establish quotas
    C. one cannot delegate authority that one does not possess
    D. the meeting of quotas should not be delegated

KEY (CORRECT ANSWERS)

1.	A		11.	A
2.	C		12.	B
3.	A		13.	D
4.	C		14.	B
5.	C		15.	A
6.	B		16.	C
7.	D		17.	D
8.	B		18.	D
9.	B		19.	B
10.	C		20.	B

21.	C
22.	B
23.	D
24.	B
25.	C

TEST 3

DIRECTIONS: Each question or incomplete statement is followed by several suggested answers or completions. Select the one that BEST answers the question or completes the statement. *PRINT THE LETTER OF THE CORRECT ANSWER IN THE SPACE AT THE RIGHT.*

1. A danger which exists in any organization as complex as that required for administration of a large public agency is that each department comes to believe that it exists for its own sake.
   The one of the following which has been attempted in some organizations as a cure for this condition is to
   A. build up the departmental esprit de corps
   B. expand the functions and jurisdictions of the various departments so that better integration is possible
   C. develop a body of specialists in the various subject matter fields which cut across departmental lines
   D. delegate authority to the lowest possible echelon
   E. systematically transfer administrative personnel from one department to another

2. At best, the organization chart is ordinarily and necessarily an idealized picture of the intent of top management, a reflection of hopes and aims rather than a photograph of the operating facts within the organization.
   The one of the following which is the basic reason for this is that the organization chart
   A. does not show the flow of work within the organization
   B. speaks in terms of positions rather than of live employees
   C. frequently contains unresolved internal ambiguities
   D. is a record of past organization or proposed future organization and never a photograph of the living organization
   E. does not label the jurisdiction assigned to each component unit

3. The drag of inadequacy is always downward. The need in administration is always for the reverse; for a department head to project his thinking to the city level, for the unit chief to try to see the problems of the department.
   The inability of a city administration to recruit administrators who can satisfy this need usually results in departments characterized by
   A. disorganization   B. poor supervision
   C. circumscribed viewpoints   D. poor public relations
   E. a lack of programs

4. When, as a result of a shift in public sentiment, the elective officers of a city are changed, is it desirable for career administrators to shift ground without performing any illegal or dishonest act in order to conform to the policies of the new elective officers?
   A. *No*; the opinions and beliefs of the career officials are the result of long experience in administration and are more reliable than those of politicians

2 (#3)

    B. *Yes*; only in this way can citizens, political officials, and career administrators alike have confidence in the performance of their respective functions
    C. *No*; a top career official who is so spineless as to change his views or procedures as a result of public opinion is of little value to the public service
    D. *Yes*; legal or illegal, it is necessary that a city employee carry out the orders of his superior officers
    E. *No*; shifting ground with every change in administration will preclude the use of a constant overall policy

5. Participation in developing plans which will affect levels in the organization in addition to his own, will contribute to an individual's understanding of the entire system. When possible, this should be encouraged.
This policy is, in general,
    A. *desirable*; the maintenance of any organization depends upon individual understanding
    B. *undesirable*; employees should participate only in these activities which affect their own level, otherwise conflicts in authority may arise
    C. *desirable*; an employee's will to contribute to the maintenance of an organization depends to a great extent on the level which he occupies
    D. *undesirable*; employees can be trained more efficiently and economically in an organized training program than by participating in plan development
    E. *desirable*; it will enable the employee to make intelligent suggestions for adjustment of the plan in the future

5.____

6. Constant study should be made of the information contained in reports to isolate those elements of experience which are static, those which are variable and repetitive, and those which are variable and due to chance.
Knowledge of those elements of experience in his organization which are static or constant will enable the operating official to
    A. fix responsibility for their supervisor at a lower level
    B. revise the procedure in order to make the elements variable
    C. arrange for follow-up and periodic adjustment
    D. bring related data together
    E. provide a frame of reference within which detailed standards for measurement can be installed

6.____

7. A chief staff officer, serving as one of the immediate advisors to the department head, has demonstrated a special capacity for achieving internal agreements and for sound judgment. As a result he has been used more and more as a source of counsel and assistance by the department head. Other staff officers and line officials as well have discovered that it is wise for them to check with this colleague in advance on all problematical matters handed up to the department head.

7.____

Developments such as this are
- A. *undesirable*; they disrupt the normal lines for flow of work in an organization
- B. *desirable*; they allow an organization to make the most of its strength wherever such strength resides
- C. *undesirable*; they tend to undermine the authority of the department head and put it in the hands of a staff officer who does not have the responsibility
- D. *desirable*; they tend to resolve internal ambiguities in organization
- E. *undesirable*; they make for bad morale by causing *cutthroat* competition

8. A common difference among executives is that some are not content unless they are out in front of everything that concerns their organization, while others prefer to run things by pulling strings, by putting others out in front and by stepping into the breach only when necessary.
   Generally speaking, an advantage this latter method of operation has over the former is that it
   - A. results in a higher level of morale over a sustained period of time
   - B. gets results by exhortation and direct stimulus
   - C. makes it unnecessary to calculate integrated moves
   - D. makes the personality of the executive felt further down the line
   - E. results in the executive getting the reputation for being a good fellow

9. Administrators frequently have to get facts by interviewing people. Although the interview is a legitimate fact gathering technique, it has definite limitations which should not be overlooked.
   The one of the following which is an important limitation is that
   - A. people who are interviewed frequently answer questions with guesses rather than admit their ignorance
   - B. it is a poor way to discover the general attitude and thinking of supervisors interviewed
   - C. people sometimes hesitate to give information during an interview which they will submit in written form
   - D. it is a poor way to discover how well employees understand departmental policies
   - E. the material obtained from the interview can usually be obtained at lower cost from existing records

10. It is desirable and advantageous to leave a maximum measure of planning responsibility to operating agencies or units, rather than to remove the responsibility to a central planning staff agency.
    Adoption of the former policy (decentralized planning) would lead to
    - A. *less effective planning*; operating personnel do not have the time to make long-term plans
    - B. *more effective planning*; operating units are usually better equipped technically than any staff agency and consequently are in a better position to set up valid plans
    - C. *less effective planning*; a central planning agency has a more objective point of view than any operating agency can achieve

D. *more effective planning*; plans are conceived in terms of the existing situation and their execution is carried out with the will to succeed
E. *less effective planning*; there is little or no opportunity to check deviation from plans in the proposed set-up

Questions 11-15.

DIRECTIONS: The following sections appeared in a report on the work production of two bureaus of a department. Base your answers to Questions 11 through 15 on this information. Throughout the report, assume that each month has 4 weeks.

Each of the two bureaus maintains a chronological file. In Bureau A, every 9 months on the average, this material fills a standard legal size cabinet sufficient for 12,000 work units. In Bureau B the same type of cabinet is filled in 18 months. Each bureau maintains three complete years of information plus a current file. When the current file cabinet is filled, the cabinet containing the oldest material is emptied, the contents disposed of, and the cabinet used for current material. The similarity of these operations makes it possible to consolidate these files with little effort.

Study of the practice of using typists as filing clerks for periods when there is no typing work showed: (1) Bureau A has for the past 6 months completed a total of 1,500 filing work units a week using on the average 100 man-hours of trained file clerk time and 20 man-hours of typist time; (2) Bureau B has in the same period completed a total of 2,000 filing work units a week using on the average 125 man-hours of trained file clerk time and 60 hours of typist time. This includes all work in chronological files. Assuming that all clerks work at the same speed and that all typists work at the same speed, this indicates that work other than filing should be found for typists or that they should be given some training in the filing procedures used. It should be noted that Bureau A has not been producing the 1,600 units of technical (not filing) work per 30-day period required by Schedule K, but is at present 200 units behind. The Bureau should be allowed 3 working days to get on schedule.

11. What percentage (approximate) of the total number of filing work units completed in both units consists of the work involved in the maintenance of the chronological files?
    A. 5%   B. 10%   C. 15%   D. 20%   E. 25%

12. If the two chronological files are consolidated, the number of months which should be allowed for filling a cabinet is
    A. 2   B. 4   C. 6   D. 8   E. 14

13. The MAXIMUM number of file cabinets which can be released for other uses as a result of the consolidation recommended is
    A. 0
    B. 1
    C. 2
    D. 3
    E. not determinable on the basis of the data given

14. If all the filing work for both units is consolidated without diminution in the amount to be done and all filing work is done by trained file clerks, the number of clerks required (35-hour work week) is
    A. 4   B. 5   C. 6   D. 7   E. 8

14.____

15. In order to comply with the recommendation with respect to Schedule K, the present work production of Bureau A must be increased by
    A. 50%
    B. 100%
    C. 150%
    D. 200%
    E. an amount which is not determinable

15.____

16. A certain training program during World War II resulted in the training of thousands of supervisors in industry. The methods of this program were later successfully applied in various government agencies. The program was based upon the assumption that there is an irreducible minimum of three supervisory skills.
    The one of these skills among the following is
    A. to know how to perform the job at hand well
    B. to be able to deal personally with workers, especially face-to-face
    C. to be able to imbue workers with the will to perform the job well
    D. to know the kind of work that is done by one's unit and the policies and procedures of one's agency
    E. the *know-how* of administrative and supervisory processes

16.____

17. A comment made by an employee about a training course was, "*We never have any idea how we ae getting along in that course.*"
    The fundamental error in training methods to which this criticism points is
    A. insufficient student participation
    B. failure to develop a feeling of need or active want for the material being presented
    C. the training sessions may be too long
    D. no attempt may have been made to connect the new material with what was already known
    E. no goals have been set for the students

17.____

18. Assume that you are attending a departmental conference on efficiency ratings at which it is proposed that a man-to-man rating scale be introduced.
    You should point out that, of the following, the CHIEF weakness of the man-to-man rating scale is that
    A. it involves abstract numbers rather than concrete employee characteristics
    B. judges are unable to select their own standards for comparison
    C. the standard for comparison shifts from man-to-man for each person rated
    D. not every person rated is given the opportunity to serve as a standard for comparison
    E. standards for comparison will vary from judge to judge

18.____

19. Assume that you are conferring with a supervisor who has assigned to his subordinates efficiency ratings which you believe to be generally too low. The supervisor argues that his ratings are generally low because his subordinates are generally inferior.
    Of the following, the evidence MOST relevant to the point at issue can be secured by comparing efficiency ratings assigned by the supervisor
    A. with ratings assigned by other supervisors in the same agency
    B. this year with ratings assigned by him in previous years
    C. to men recently transferred to his unit with ratings previously earned by these men
    D. with the general city average of ratings assigned by all supervisors to all employees
    E. with the relative order of merit of his employees as determined independently by promotion test marks

20. The one of the following which is NOT among the most common of the compensable factors used in wage evaluation studies is
    A. initiative and ingenuity required
    B. physical demand
    C. responsibility for the safety of others
    D. working conditions
    E. presence of avoidable hazards

21. If independent functions are separated, there is an immediate gain in conserving special skills. If we are to make optimum use of the abilities of our employees, these skills must be conserved.
    Assuming the correctness of this statement, it follows that
    A. if we are not making optimum use of employee abilities, independent functions have not been separated
    B. we are making optimum uses of employee abilities if we conserve special skills
    C. we are making optimum use of employee abilities if independent functions have been separated
    D. we are not making optimum use of employee abilities if we do not conserve special skills
    E. if special skills are being conserved, independent functions need not be separated

22. A reorganization of the bureau to provide for a stenographic pool instead of individual unit stenographers will result in more stenographic help being available to each unit when it is required, and consequently will result in greater productivity for each unit. An analysis of the space requirements shows that setting up a stenographic pool will require a minimum of 400 square feet of good space. In order to obtain this space, it will be necessary to reduce the space available for technical personnel, resulting in lesser productivity for each unit.

On the basis of the above discussion, it can be stated that, in order to obtain greater productivity for each unit,
- A. a stenographic pool should be set up
- B. further analysis of the space requirement should be made
- C. it is not certain as to whether or not a stenographic pool should be set up
- D. the space available for each technician should be increased in order to compensate for the absence of a stenographic pool
- E. a stenographic pool should not be set up

23. The adoption of single consolidated form will mean that most of the form will not be used in any one operation. This would create waste and confusion. This conclusion is based upon the unstated hypothesis that
- A. if waste and confusion are to be avoided, a single consolidated form should be used
- B. if a single consolidated form is constructed, most of it can be used in each operation
- C. if waste and confusion are to be avoided, most of the form employed should be used
- D. most of a single consolidation form is not used
- E. a single consolidated form should not be used

23.____

KEY (CORRECT ANSWERS)

1.	E		11.	C
2.	B		12.	C
3.	C		13.	B
4.	B		14.	D
5.	E		15.	E
6.	A		16.	B
7.	B		17.	E
8.	A		18.	E
9.	A		19.	C
10.	D		20.	E

21. D
22. C
23. C

COMMUNICATION

EXAMINATION SECTION
TEST 1

DIRECTIONS: Each question or incomplete statement is followed by several suggested answers or completions. Select the one that BEST answers the question or completes the statement. *PRINT THE LETTER OF THE CORRECT ANSWER IN THE SPACE AT THE RIGHT.*

1. In some agencies the counsel to the agency head is given the right to bypass the chain of command and issue orders directly to the staff concerning matters that involve certain specific processes and practices.
   This situation MOST nearly illustrates the principle of _____ authority.
   A. the acceptance theory of
   B. multiple-linear
   C. splintered
   D. functional

2. It is commonly understood that communication is an important part of the administrative process.
   Which of the following is NOT a valid principle of the communication process in administration?
   A. The channels of communication should be spontaneous.
   B. The lines of communication should be as direct and as short as possible.
   C. Communications should be authenticated.
   D. The persons serving in communications centers should be competent.

3. Of the following, the one factor which is generally considered LEAST essential to successful committee operations is
   A. stating a clear definition of the authority and scope of the committee
   B. selecting the committee chairman carefully
   C. limiting the size of the committee to four persons
   D. limiting the subject matter to that which can be handled in group discussion

4. Of the following, the failure by line managers to accept and appreciate the benefits and limitations of a new program or system VERY FREQUENTLY can be traced to the
   A. budgetary problems involved
   B. resultant need to reduce staff
   C. lack of controls it engenders
   D. failure of top management to support its implementation

5. If a manager were thinking about using a committee of subordinates to solve an operating problem, which of the following would generally NOT be an advantage of such use of the committee approach?
   A. Improved coordination
   B. Low cost
   C. Increased motivation
   D. Integrated judgment

6. Every supervisor has many occasions to lead a conference or participate in a conference of some sort.
Of the following statements that pertain to conferences and conference leadership, which is generally considered to be MOST valid?
   A. Since World War II, the trend has been toward fewer shared decisions and more conferences.
   B. The most important part of a conference leader's job is to direct discussion.
   C. In providing opportunities for group interaction, management should avoid consideration of its past management philosophy.
   D. A good administrator cannot lead a good conference if he is a poor public speaker.

7. Of the following, it is usually LEAST desirable for a conference leader to
   A. call the name of a person after asking a question
   B. summarize proceedings periodically
   C. make a practice of repeating questions
   D. ask a question without indicating who is to reply

8. Assume that, in a certain organization, a situation has developed in which there is little difference in status or authority between individuals.
Which of the following would be the MOST likely result with regard to communication in this organization?
   A. Both the accuracy and flow of communication will be improved.
   B. Both the accuracy and flow of communication will substantially decrease.
   C. Employees will seek more formal lines of communication.
   D. Neither the flow nor the accuracy of communication will be improved over the former hierarchical structure.

9. The main function of many agency administrative officers is "information management." Information that is received by an administrative officer may be classified as active or passive, depending upon whether or not it requires the recipient to take some action.
Of the following, the item received which is clearly the MOST active information is
   A. an appointment of a new staff member
   B. a payment voucher for a new desk
   C. a press release concerning a past event
   D. the minutes of a staff meeting

10. Of the following, the one LEAST considered to be a communication barrier is
    A. group feedback   B. charged words
    C. selective perception   D. symbolic meanings

11. Management studies support the hypothesis that, in spite of the tendency of employees to censor the information communicated to their supervisor, subordinates are more likely to communicate problem-oriented information UPWARD when they have a
    A. long period of service in the organization
    B. high degree of trust in the supervisor
    C. high educational level
    D. low status on the organizational ladder

11.____

12. Electronic data processing equipment can produce more information faster than can be generated by any other means.
    In view of this, the MOST important problem faced by management at present is to
    A. keep computers fully occupied
    B. find enough computer personnel
    C. assimilate and properly evaluate the information
    D. obtain funds to establish appropriate information systems

12.____

13. A well-designed management information system essentially provides each executive and manager the information he needs for
    A. determining computer time requirements
    B. planning and measuring results
    C. drawing a new organization chart
    D. developing a new office layout

13.____

14. It is generally agreed that management policies should be periodically reappraised and restated in accordance with current conditions.
    Of the following, the approach which would be MOST effective in determining whether a policy should be revised is to
    A. conduct interviews with staff members at all levels in order to ascertain the relationship between the policy and actual practice
    B. make proposed revisions in the policy and apply it to current problems
    C. make up hypothetical situations using both the old policy and a revised version in order to make comparisons
    D. call a meeting of top level staff in order to discuss ways of revising the policy

14.____

15. Your superior has asked you to notify division employees of an important change in one of the operating procedures described in the division manual. Every employee presently has a copy of this manual.
    Which of the following is normally the MOST practical way to get the employees to understand such a change?
    A. Notify each employee individually of the change and answer any questions he might have
    B. Send a written notice to key personnel, directing them to inform the people under them

15.____

C. Call a general meeting, distribute a corrected page for the manual, and discuss the change
D. Send a memo to employees describing the change in general terms and asking them to make the necessary corrections in their copies of the manual

16. Assume that the work in your department involves the use of any technical terms.
   In such a situation, when you are answering inquiries from the general public, it would usually be BEST to
   A. use simple language and avoid the technical terms
   B. employ the technical terms whenever possible
   C. bandy technical terms freely, but explain each term in parentheses
   D. apologize if you are forced to use a technical term

16._____

17. Suppose that you receive a telephone call from someone identifying himself as an employee in another city department who asks to be given information which your own department regards as confidential.
   Which of the following is the BEST way of handling such a request?
   A. Give the information requested, since your caller as official standing
   B. Grant the request, provided the caller gives you a signed receipt
   C. Refuse the request, because you have no way of knowing whether the caller is really who he claims to be
   D. Explain that the information is confidential and inform the caller of the channels he must go through to have the information released to him

17._____

18. Studies show that office employees place high importance on the social and human aspects of the organization. What office employees like best about their jobs is the kind of people with whom they work. So strive hard to group people who are most likely to get along well together.
   Based on this information, it is MOST reasonable to assume that office workers are most pleased to work in a group which
   A. is congenial   B. has high productivity
   C. allows individual creativity   D. is unlike other groups

18._____

19. A certain supervisor does not compliment members of his staff when they come up with good ideas. He feels that coming up with good ideas is part of the job and does not merit special attention.
   This supervisor's practice is
   A. *poor*, because recognition for good ideas is a good motivator
   B. *poor*, because the staff will suspect that the supervisor has no good ideas of his own
   C. *good*, because it is reasonable to assume that employees will tell their supervisor of ways to improve office practice
   D. *good*, because the other members of the staff are not made to seem inferior by comparison

19._____

20. Some employees of a department have sent an anonymous letter containing many complaints to the department head.
    Of the following, what is this MOST likely to show about the department?
    A. It is probably a good place to work.
    B. Communications are probably poor.
    C. The complaints are probably unjustified.
    D. These employees are probably untrustworthy.

21. Which of the following actions would usually be MOST appropriate for a supervisor to take after receiving an instruction sheet from his superior explaining a new procedure which is to be followed?
    A. Put the instruction sheet aside temporarily until he determines what is wrong with the old procedure.
    B. Call his superior and ask whether the procedure is one he must implement immediately.
    C. Write a memorandum to the superior asking for more details.
    D. Try the new procedure and advise the superior of any problems or possible improvements.

22. Of the following, which one is considered the PRIMARY advantage of using a committee to resolved a problem in an organization?
    A. No one person will be held accountable for the decision since a group of people was involved.
    B. People with different backgrounds give attention to the problem.
    C. The decision will take considerable time so there is unlikely to be a decision that will later be regretted.
    D. One person cannot dominate the decision-making process.

23. Employees in a certain office come to their supervisor with all their complaints about the office and the work. Almost every employee has had at least one minor complaint at some time.
    The situation with respect to complaints in this office may BEST be described as probably
    A. *good*; employees who complain care about their jobs and work hard
    B. *good*; grievances brought out into the open can be corrected
    C. *bad*; only serious complaints should be discussed
    D. *bad*; it indicates the staff does not have confidence in the administration

24. The administrator who allows his staff to suggest ways to do their work will usually find that
    A. this practice contributes to high productivity
    B. the administrator's ideas produce greater output
    C. clerical employees suggest inefficient work methods
    D. subordinate employees resent performing a management function

25. The MAIN purpose for a supervisor's questioning the employees at a conference he is holding is to
    A. stress those areas of information covered but not understood by the participants
    B. encourage participants to think through the problem under discussion
    C. catch those subordinates who are not paying attention
    D. permit the more knowledgeable participants to display their grasp of the problems being discussed

25.____

KEY (CORRECT ANSWERS)

1. D
2. A
3. C
4. D
5. B

6. B
7. C
8. D
9. A
10. A

11. B
12. C
13. B
14. A
15. C

16. A
17. D
18. A
19. A
20. B

21. D
22. B
23. B
24. A
25. B

TEST 2

DIRECTIONS: Each question or incomplete statement is followed by several suggested answers or completions. Select the one that BEST answers the question or completes the statement. *PRINT THE LETTER OF THE CORRECT ANSWER IN THE SPACE AT THE RIGHT.*

1. For a superior to use *consultative supervision* with his subordinates effectively, it is ESSENTIAL that he
   A. accept the fact that his formal authority will be weakened by the procedure
   B. admit that he does not know more than all his men together and that his ideas are not always best
   C. utilize a committee system so that the procedure is orderly
   D. make sure that all subordinates are consulted so that no one feels left out

   1.____

2. The *grapevine* is an informal means of communication in an organization. The attitude of a supervisor with respect to the grapevine should be to
   A. ignore it since it deals mainly with rumors and sensational information
   B. regard it as a serious danger which should be eliminated
   C. accept it as a real line of communication which should be listened to
   D. utilize it for most purposes instead of the official line of communication

   2.____

3. The supervisor of an office that must deal with the public should realize that planning in this type of work situation
   A. is useless because he does not know how many people will request service or what service they will request
   B. must be done at a higher level but that he should be ready to implement the results of such planning
   C. is useful primarily for those activities that are not concerned with public contact
   D. is useful for all the activities of the office, including those that relate to public contact

   3.____

4. Assume that it is your job to receive incoming telephone calls. Those calls which you cannot handle yourself have to be transferred to the appropriate office.
   If you receive an outside call for an extension line which is busy, the one of the following which you should do FIRST is to
   A. interrupt the person speaking on the extension and tell him a call is waiting
   B. tell the caller the line is busy and let him know every thirty seconds whether or not it is free
   C. leave the caller on "hold" until the extension is free
   D. tell the caller the line is busy and ask him if he wishes to wait

   4.____

2 (#2)

5. Your superior has subscribed to several publications directly related to your division's work, and he has asked you to see to it that the publications are circulated among the supervisory personnel in the division. There are eight supervisors involved.
   The BEST method of insuring that all eight see these publications is to
   A. place the publication in the division's general reference library as soon as it arrives
   B. inform each supervisor whenever a publication arrives and remind all of them that they are responsible for reading it
   C. prepare a standard slip that can be stapled to each publication, listing the eight supervisors and saying, "Please read, initial your name, and pass along"
   D. send a memo to the eight supervisors saying that they may wish to purchase individual subscriptions in their own names if they are interested in seeing each issue

5._____

6. Your superior has telephoned a number of key officials in your agency to ask whether they can meet at a certain time next month. He has found that they can all make it, and he has asked you to confirm the meeting.
   Which of the following is the BEST way to confirm such a meeting?
   A. Note the meeting on your superior's calendar.
   B. Post a notice of the meeting on the agency bulletin board.
   C. Call the officials on the day of the meeting to remind them of the meeting.
   D. Write a memo to each official involved, repeating the time and place of the meeting.

6._____

7. Assume that a new city regulation requires that certain kinds of private organizations file information forms with your department. You have been asked to write the short explanatory message that will be printed on the front cover of the pamphlet containing the forms and instructions.
   Which of the following would be the MOST appropriate way of beginning this message?
   A. Get the readers' attention by emphasizing immediately that there are legal penalties for organizations that fail to file before a certain date.
   B. Briefly state the nature of the enclosed forms and the types of organizations that must file.
   C. Say that your department is very sorry to have to put organizations to such an inconvenience.
   D. Quote the entire regulation adopted by the city, even if it is quite long and is expressed din complicated legal language.

7._____

8. Suppose that you have been told to make up the vacation schedule for the 18 employees in a particular unit. In order for the unit to operate effectively, only a few employees can be on vacation at the same time.
   Which of the following is the MOST advisable approach in making up the schedule?
   A. Draw up a schedule assigning vacations in alphabetical order
   B. Find out when the supervisors want to take their vacations, and randomly assign whatever periods are left to the non-supervisory personnel

8._____

C. Assign the most desirable times to employees of longest standing and the least desirable times to the newest employees
D. Have all employees state their own preference, and then work out any conflicts in consultation with the people involved

9. Assume that you have been asked to prepare job descriptions for various positions in your department.
Which of the following are the basic points that should be covered in a *job description*?
   A. General duties and responsibilities of the position, with examples of day-to-day tasks
   B. Comments on the performances of present employees
   C. Estimates of the number of openings that may be available in each category during the coming year
   D. Instructions for carrying out the specific tasks assigned to your department

10. Of the following, the biggest DISADVANTAGE in allowing a free flow of communications in an agency is that such a free flow
    A. decreases creativity
    B. increases the use of the *grapevine*
    C. lengthens the chain of command
    D. reduces the executive's power to direct the flow of information

11. A downward flow of authority in an organization is one example of _____ communication.
    A. horizontal   B. informal   C. circular   D. vertical

12. Of the following, the one that would MOST likely block effective communication is
    A. concentration only on the issues at hand
    B. lack of interest or commitment
    C. use of written reports
    D. use of charts and graphs

13. An ADVANTAGE of the *lecture* as a teaching tool is that it
    A. enables a person to present his ideas to a large number of people
    B. allows the audience to retain a maximum of the information given
    C. holds the attention of the audience for the longest time
    D. enables the audience member to easily recall the main points

14. An ADVANTAGE of the *small-group* discussion as a teaching tool is that
    A. it always focuses attention on one person as the leader
    B. it places collective responsibility on the group as a whole
    C. its members gain experience by summarizing the ideas of others
    D. each member of the group acts as a member of a team

15. The one of the following that is an ADVANTAGE of a *large-group* discussion, when compared to a small-group discussion, is that the large-group discussion
    A. moves along more quickly than a small-group discussion
    B. allows its participants to feel more at ease, and speak out more freely
    C. gives the whole group a chance to exchange ideas on a certain subject at the same occasion
    D. allows its members to feel a greater sense of personal responsibility

15.____

KEY (CORRECT ANSWERS)

1.	D	6.	D	11.	D
2.	C	7.	B	12.	B
3.	D	8.	D	13.	A
4.	D	9.	A	14.	D
5.	C	10.	D	15.	C

READING COMPREHENSION
UNDERSTANDING AND INTERPRETING WRITTEN MATERIAL
EXAMINATION SECTION

This exam section includes some passages and questions related to functions of the first computerized offices, which consisted of typewriters and other such manual office equipment.

TEST 1

DIRECTIONS: Each question or incomplete statement is followed by several suggested answers or completions. Select the one that BEST answers the question or completes the statement. *PRINT THE LETTER OF THE CORRECT ANSWER IN THE SPACE AT THE RIGHT.*

Questions 1-2.

DIRECTIONS: Questions 1 and 2 are to be answered SOLELY on the basis of the following passage.

The employees in a unit or division of a government agency may be referred to as a work group. Within a government agency which has existed for some time, the work groups will have evolved traditions of their own. The persons in these work groups acquire these traditions as part of the process of work adjustment within their groups. Usually, a work group in a large organization will contain *oldtimers*, *newcomers*, and *in-betweeners*. Like the supervisor of a group, who is not necessarily an oldtimer or the oldest member, oldtimers usually have great influence. They can recall events unknown to others and are a storehouse of information and advice about current problems in the light of past experience. They pass along the traditions of the group to the others who, in turn, become oldtimers themselves. Thus, the traditions of the group which have been honored and revered by long acceptance are continued.

1. According to the above passage, the traditions of a work group within a government agency are developed
    A. at the time the group is established
    B. over a considerable period of time
    C. in order to give recognition to oldtimers
    D. for the group before it is established

    1._____

2. According to the above passage, the oldtimers within a work group
    A. are the means by which long accepted practices and customs are perpetuated
    B. would best be able to settle current problems that arise
    C. are honored because of the changes they have made in the traditions
    D. have demonstrated that they have learned to do their work well

    2._____

Questions 3-4.

DIRECTIONS: Questions 3 and 4 are to be answered SOLELY on the following passage.

In public agencies, the success of a person assigned to perform first-line supervisory duties depends in large part upon the personal relations between him and his subordinate employees. The goal of supervising effort is something more than to obtain compliance with procedures established by some central office. The major objective is work accomplishment. In order for this goal to be attained, employees must want to attain it and must exercise initiative in their work. Only if employees are generally satisfied with the type of supervision which exists in an organization will they put forth their best efforts.

3. According to the above passage, in order for employees to try to do their work as well as they can, it is essential that
    A. they participate in determining their working conditions and rates of pay
    B. their supervisors support the employees' viewpoints in meetings with higher management
    C. they are content with the supervisory practices which are being used
    D. their supervisors make the changes in working procedures that the employees request

4. It can be inferred from the above passage that the goals of a unit in a public agency will not be reached unless the employees in the unit
    A. wish to reach them and are given the opportunity to make individual contributions to the work
    B. understand the relationship between the goals of the unit and goals of the agency
    C. have satisfactory personal relationships with employees of other units in the agency
    D. carefully follow the directions issued by higher authorities

Questions 5-9.

DIRECTIONS: Questions 5 through 9 are to be answered SOLELY on the basis of the following passage.

In an employee thinks he can save money, time, or material for the city or has an idea about how to do something better than it is being done, he shouldn't keep it to himself. He should send his ideas to the Employees' Suggestion Program, using the special form which is kept on hand in all departments. An employee may send in as many ideas as he wishes. To make sure that each idea is judged fairly, the name of the suggester is not made known until an award is made. The awards are certificate of merit or cash prizes ranging from $10 to $500.

5. According to the above passage, an employee who knows how to do a job in a better way should
    A. be sure it saves enough time to be worthwhile
    B. get paid the money he saves for the city
    C. keep it to himself to avoid being accused of causing a speed-up
    D. send his idea to the Employees' Suggestion Program

6. In order to send his idea to the Employees' Suggestion Program, an employee should
    A. ask the Department of Personnel for a special form
    B. get the special form in his own department
    C. mail the idea using Special Delivery
    D. send it on plain, white letter-size paper

6._____

7. An employee may send to the Employees' Suggestion Program
    A. as many ideas as he can think of
    B. no more than one idea each week
    C. no more than ten ideas in a month
    D. only one idea on each part of the job

7._____

8. The reason the name of an employee who makes a suggestion is not made known at first is to
    A. give the employee a larger award
    B. help the judges give more awards
    C. insure fairness in judging
    D. only one idea on each part of the job

8._____

9. An employee whose suggestion receives an award may be given a
    A. bonus once a year
    B. certificate for $10
    C. cash prize of up to $500
    D. salary increase of $500

9._____

Questions 10-12.

DIRECTIONS: Questions 10 through 12 are to be answered SOLELY on the basis of the following passage.

According to the rules of the Department of Personnel, the work of every permanent city employee is reviewed and rated by his supervisor at least once a year. The civil service rating system gives the employee and his supervisor a chance to talk about the progress made during the past year as well as about those parts of the job in which the employee needs to do better. In order to receive a pay increase each year, the employee must have a satisfactory service rating. Service ratings also count toward an employee's final mark on a promotion examination.

10. According to the above passage, a permanent city employee is rated AT LEAST once
    A. before his work is reviewed
    B. every six months
    C. yearly by his supervisor
    D. yearly by the Department of Personnel

10._____

11. According to the above passage, under the rating system the supervisor and the employee can discuss how
    A. much more work needs to be done next year
    B. the employee did his work last year
    C. the work can be made easier next year
    D. the work of the Department can be increased

11._____

12. According to the above passage, a permanent city employee will NOT receive a yearly pay increase
    A. if he received a pay increase the year before
    B. if he used his service rating for his mark on a promotion examination
    C. if his service rating is unsatisfactory
    D. unless he got some kind of a service rating

Questions 13-16.

DIRECTIONS: Questions 13 through 16 are to be answered SOLELY on the basis of the following passage.

It is an accepted fact that the rank and file employee can frequently advance worthwhile suggestions toward increasing efficiency. For this reason, an Employees' Suggestion System has been developed and put into operation. Suitable means have been provided at each departmental location for the confidential submission of suggestions. Numerous suggestions have been received thus far and, after study, about five percent of the ideas submitted are being translated into action. It is planned to set up, eventually, monetary awards for all worthwhile suggestions.

13. According to the above passage, a MAJOR reason why an Employees' Suggestion System was established is that
    A. an organized program of improvement is better than a haphazard one
    B. employees can often give good suggestions to increase efficiency
    C. once a fact is accepted, it is better to act on it than to do nothing
    D. the suggestions of rank and file employees were being neglected

14. According to the above passage, under the Employees' Suggestion System,
    A. a file of worthwhile suggestions will eventually be set up at each departmental location
    B. it is possible for employees to turn in suggestions without fellow employees knowing of it
    C. means have been provided for the regular and frequent collection of suggestions submitted
    D. provision has been made for the judging of worthwhile suggestions by an Employees' Suggestion Committee

15. According to the above passage, it is reasonable to assume that
    A. all suggestions must be turned in at a central office
    B. employees who make worthwhile suggestions will be promoted
    C. not all the prizes offered will be monetary ones
    D. prizes of money will be given for the best suggestions

16. According to the above passage, of the many suggestions made,
    A. all are first tested   B. a small part are put into use
    C. most are very worthwhile   D. samples are studied

Questions 17-20.

DIRECTIONS: Questions 17 through 20 are to be answered SOLELY on the basis of the following passage.

Employees may be granted leaves of absence without pay at the discretion of the Personnel Officer. Such a leave without pay shall begin on the first working day on which the employee does not report for duty and shall continue to the first day on which the employee returns to duty. The Personnel Division may vary the dates of the leave for the record so as to conform with payroll periods, but in no case shall an employee be off the payroll for a different number of calendar days than would have been the case if the actual dates mentioned above had been used. An employee who has vacation or overtime to his credit, which is available for normal use, may take time off immediately prior to beginning a leave of absence without pay, chargeable against all or part of such vacation or overtime.

17. According to the above passage, the Personnel Officer must
    A. decide if a leave of absence without pay should be granted
    B. require that a leave end on the last working day of a payroll period
    C. see to it that a leave of absence to conform with a payroll period
    D. vary the dates of a leave of absence to conform with a payroll period

18. According to the above passage, the exact dates of a leave of absence without pay may be varied provided that the
    A. calendar days an employee is off the payroll equal the actual leave granted
    B. leave conforms to an even number of payroll periods
    C. leave when granted made provision for variance to simplify payroll records
    D. Personnel Officer approves the variation

19. According to the above passage, a leave of absence without pay must extend from the
    A. first day of a calendar period to the first day the employee resumes work
    B. first day of a payroll period to the last calendar day of the leave
    C. first working day missed to the first day on which the employee resumes work
    D. last day on which an employee works through the first day he returns to work

20. According to the above passage, an employee may take extra time off just before the start of a leave of absence without pay if
    A. he charges this extra time against his leave
    B. he has a favorable balance of vacation or overtime which has been frozen
    C. the vacation or overtime that he would normally use for a leave without pay has not been charged in this way before
    D. there is time to his credit which he may use

Question 21.

DIRECTIONS: Question 21 is to be answered SOLELY on the basis of the following passage.

In considering those things which are motivators and incentives to work, it might be just as erroneous not to give sufficient weight to money as an incentive as it is to give too much weight. It is not a problem of establishing a rank-order of importance, but one of knowing that motivation is a blend or mixture rather than a pure element. It is simple to say that cultural factors count more than financial considerations, but this leads only to the conclusion that our society is financial-oriented.

21. Based on the above passage, in our society, cultural and social motivations to work are   21._____
    A. things which cannot be avoided
    B. melded to financial incentives
    C. of less consideration than high pay
    D. not balanced equally with economic or financial considerations

Question 22.

DIRECTIONS: Question 22 is to be answered SOLELY on the basis of the following passage.

A general principle of training and learning with respect to people is that they learn more readily if they receive *feedback*. Essential to maintaining proper motivational levels is knowledge of results which indicate level of progress. Feedback also assists the learning process by identifying mistakes. If this kind of information were not given to the learner, then improper or inappropriate job performance may be instilled.

22. Based on the above passage, which of the following is MOST accurate?   22._____
    A. Learning will not take place without feedback.
    B. In the absence of feedback, improper or inappropriate job performance will be learned.
    C. To properly motivate a learner, the learner must have his progress made known to him.
    D. Trainees should be told exactly what to do if they are to learn properly

Questions 23.

DIRECTIONS: Question 23 is to be answered SOLELY on the basis of the following passage.

In a democracy, the obligation of public officials is twofold. They must not only do an efficient and satisfactory job of administration, but also they must persuade the public that it is an efficient and satisfactory job. It is a burden which, if properly assumed, will make democracy work and perpetuate reform government.

23. The above passage means that   23._____
    A. public officials should try to please everybody

B. public opinion is instrumental if determining the policy of public officials
C. satisfactory performance of the job of administration will eliminate opposition to its work
D. frank and open procedure in a public agency will aid in maintaining progressive government

Question 24.

DIRECTIONS: Question 24 is to be answered SOLELY on the basis of the following passage.

Upon retirement for service, a member shall receive a retirement allowance which shall consist of an annuity which shall be the actuarial equivalent of his accumulated deductions at the time of his retirement and a pension, in addition to his annuity, which shall be equal to one service-fraction of his final compensation, multiplied by the number of years of service since he last became a member credited to him, and a pension which is the actuarial equivalent of the reserve-for-increased-take-home-pay to which he may then be entitled, if any.

24. According to the above passage, a retirement allowance shall consist of a(n)   24.____
    A. annuity, plus a pension, plus an actuarial equivalent
    B. annuity, plus a pension, plus reserve-for-increased-take-home-pay, if any
    C. annuity, plus reserve-for-increased-take-home-pay, if any, plus final compensation
    D. pension, plus reserve-for-increased-take-home-pay, if any, plus accumulated deductions

Question 25.

DIRECTIONS: Question 25 is to be answered SOLELY on the basis of the following passage.

Membership in the retirement system shall cease upon the occurrence of any one of the following conditions: when the time out of service of any member who has total service of less than 25 years, shall aggregate more than 5 years; when the time out of service of any member who has total service of 25 years or more, shall aggregate more than 10 years; when any member shall have withdrawn more than 50% of his accumulated deductions; or when any member shall have withdrawn the cash benefit provided by Section B3.35.0 of the Administrative Code.

25. According to the information in the above passage, membership in the   25.____
    retirement system shall cease when an employee
    A. with 17 years of service has been on a leave of absence for 3 years
    B. withdraws 50% of his accumulated deductions
    C. with 28 years of service has been out of service for 10 years
    D. withdraws his cash benefits

KEY (CORRECT ANSWERS)

1. B
2. A
3. C
4. A
5. D

6. B
7. A
8. C
9. B
10. C

11. B
12. C
13. B
14. B
15. D

16. B
17. A
18. A
19. C
20. D

21. B
22. C
23. D
24. B
25. D

TEST 2

DIRECTIONS: Each question or incomplete statement is followed by several suggested answers or completions. Select the one that BEST answers the question or completes the statement. *PRINT THE LETTER OF THE CORRECT ANSWER IN THE SPACE AT THE RIGHT.*

Questions 1-6.

DIRECTIONS: Questions 1 through 6 are to be answered SOLELY on the basis of the following passage.

Since almost every office has some contact with data-processed records, a stenographer should have some understanding of the basic operations of data processing. Data processing systems now handle a vast majority of all office paperwork. On coded forms and other specialized media, data are recorded before being fed into the computer for processing. The data written on the source document is converted in highly advanced ways in order to make the information accessible to the user. After data has been converted, it must be verified to guarantee absolute accuracy. In this manner, data becomes a permanent record which can be read by computers that compare, store, compute, and otherwise process data at high speeds.

One key person in a computer installation is a programmer, the man or woman who puts business and scientific problems into special symbolic languages that can be read by the computer. Jobs done by the computer range all the way from payroll operations to chemical process control, but most computer applications are directed toward management data. Most programmers employed by business come to their positions with college degrees; the rest are promoted to their positions from within the organization on the basis of demonstrated ability without regard to education.

1. Of the following, the BEST title for the above passage is
    A. The Stenographer As Data Processor
    B. The Relation of Data Input to Stenography
    C. Understanding Data Processing
    D. Permanent Office Records

2. According to the above passage, a stenographer should understand the basic operations of data processing because
    A. almost every office today has contact with data processed by computer
    B. any office worker may be asked to verify the accuracy of data
    C. most offices are involved in the production of permanent records
    D. data may be converted into computer language by specialized media

3. According to the above passage, data accuracy is reviewed during the _____ stage.
    A. processing
    B. verification
    C. programming
    D. stenographic

4. According to the above passage, computers are used MOST often to handle
   A. management data
   B. problems of higher education
   C. the control of chemical processes
   D. payroll operations

5. Computer programming is taught in many colleges and business schools. The above passage implies that programmers in industry
   A. must have professional training
   B. need professional training to advance
   C. must have at least a college education to do adequate programming tasks
   D. do not necessarily need college education to do programming work

6. According to the above passage, data to be processed by computer should be
   A. recent   B. basic   C. complete   D. verified

Questions 7-10.

DIRECTIONS: Questions 7 through 10 are to be answered SOLELY on the basis of the following passage.

There is nothing that will take the place of good sense on the part of the stenographer. You may be perfect in transcribing exactly what the dictator says and your speed may be adequate, but without an understanding of the dictator's intent as well as his words, you are likely to be a mediocre secretary.

A serious error that is made when taking dictation is putting down something that does not make sense. Most people who dictate material would rather be asked to repeat and explain than to receive transcribed material which has errors due to inattention or doubt. Many dictators request that their grammar be corrected by their secretaries, but unless specifically asked to do so, secretaries should not do it without first checking with the dictator. Secretaries should be aware that, in some cases, dictators may use incorrect grammar or slang expressions to create a particular effect.

Some people dictate commas, periods, and paragraphs, while others expect the stenographer to know when, where, and how to punctuate. A well-trained secretary should be able to indicate the proper punctuation by listening to the pauses and tones of the dictator's voice.

A stenographer who has taken dictation from the same person for a period of time should be able to understand him under most conditions. By increasing her tack, alertness, and efficiency, a secretary can become more competent.

7. According to the above passage, which of the following statements concerning the dictation of punctuation is CORRECT?
   A. Dictator may use incorrect punctuation to create a desired style.
   B. Dictator should indicate all punctuation.

C. Stenographer should know how to punctuate based on the pauses and tones of the dictator.
D. Stenographer should not type any punctuation if it has not been dictated to her.

8. According to the above passage, how should secretaries handle grammatical errors in a dictation?
Secretaries should
    A. *not correct* grammatical errors unless the dictator is aware that this is being done
    B. *correct* grammatical errors by having the dictator repeat the line with proper pauses
    C. *correct* grammatical errors if they have checked the correctness in a grammar book
    D. *correct* grammatical errors based on their own good sense

8.____

9. If a stenographer is confused about the method of spacing and indenting of a report which has just been dictated to her, she GENERALLY should
    A. do the best she can
    B. ask the dictator to explain what she should do
    C. try to improve her ability to understand dictated material
    D. accept the fact that her stenographic ability is not adequate

9.____

10. In the last line of the first paragraph, the word *mediocre* means MOST NEARLY
    A. superior   B. respected   C. disregarded   D. second-rate

10.____

Questions 11-12.

DIRECTIONS: Questions 11 and 12 are to be answered SOLELY on the basis of the following passage.

The number of legible carbon copies required to be produced determines the weight of the carbon paper to be used. When only one copy is made, heavy carbon paper is satisfactory. Most typists, however, use medium-weight carbon paper and find it serviceable for up to three or four copies. If five or more copies are to be made, it is wise to use light carbon paper. On the other hand, the finish of carbon paper to be used depends largely on the stroke of the typist and, in lesser degree, on the number of copies to be made and on whether the typewriter has pica or elite type. A soft-finish carbon paper should be used if the typist's touch is light or if a noiseless machine is used. It is desirable for the average typist to use medium-finish carbon paper for ordinary work, when only a few carbon copies are required. Elite type requires a harder carbon finish than pica type for the same number of copies.

11. According to the above passage, the lighter the carbon paper used, the
    A. softer the finish of the carbon paper will be
    B. greater the number of legible carbon copies that can be made
    C. greater the number of times the carbon paper can be used
    D. lighter the typist's touch should be

11.____

12. According to the above passage, the MOST important factor which determines whether the finish of carbon paper to be used in typing should be hard, medium, or soft is
    A. the touch of the typist
    B. the number of carbon copies required
    C. whether the type in the typewriter is pica or elite
    D. whether a machine with pica type will produce the same number of carbon copies as a machine with elite type

Questions 13-16.

DIRECTIONS: Questions 13 through 16 are to be answered SOLELY on the basis of the following passage.

Looking back at past developments in office work, advances were made at higher speeds and at greater efficiency thanks largely to the typewriter. The typewriter was a substitute for handwriting and, in the hands of a skilled typist, not only turned out letters and other documents at least three times faster than a penman, but turned out the greater volume more uniformly and legibly. With the use of carbon paper and onionskin paper, identical copies could be made at the same time.

The typewriter, besides its effect on the conduct of business and government, had a very important effect on the position of women. The typewriter did much to bring women into business and government, and in a short time span, women far outnumbered men as typists. Many women used the keys of the typewriter to climb the ladder to professional managerial positions.

The typewriter, as its name implies, employs type to make an ink impression on paper. For many years, the manual typewriter was the standard machine used. Eventually, the electric typewriter became dominant, leading to innovations in and widespread use of completely automatic electronic typewriters.

The mechanism of the office manual typewriter includes a set of keys arranged systematically in rows; a semicircular frame of type, connected to the keys by levers; the carriage, or paper carrier; a rubber roller, called a platen, against which the type strikes; and an inked ribbon which makes the impression of the type character when the key strikes it.

13. The above passage mentions a number of good features of the combination of a skilled typist and a typewriter.
    Of the following the feature which is NOT mentioned in the passage is
    A. speed   B. reliability   C. uniformity   D. legibility

14. According to the above passage, a skilled typist can
    A. turn out at least five carbon copies of typed matter
    B. type at least three times faster than a penman can write
    C. type more than 80 words in a minute
    D. readily move into a managerial position

15. According to the above passage, which of the following is NOT part of the mechanism of a manual typewriter?
    A. Carbon paper
    B. Platen
    C. Paper carrier
    D. Inked ribbon

15.____

16. According to the above passage, the typewriter helped
    A. men more than women in business
    B. women in career advancement into management
    C. men and women equally, but women have taken better advantage of it
    D. more women than men, because men generally dislike routine typing work

16.____

Questions 17-21.

DIRECTIONS: Questions 17 through 21 are to be answered SOLELY on the basis of the following passage.

The recipient gains an impression of a typewritten letter before he begins to read the message. Factors which provide for a good first impression include margins and spacing that are visually pleasing, formal parts of the letter which are correctly placed according to the style of the letter, copy which is free of obvious erasures and over-strikes, and transcript that is even and clear. The problem for the typist is that of how to produce that first, positive impression of her work.

There are several general rules which a typist can follow when she wishes to prepare a properly spaced letter on a sheet of letterhead. Ordinarily, the width of a letter should not be less than four inches nor more than six inches. The side margins should also have a desirable relation to the bottom margin and the space between the letterhead and the body of the letter. Usually the most appealing arrangement is when the side margins are even and the bottom margin is slightly wider than the side margins. In some offices, however, standard line length is used for all business letter, and the secretary then varies the spacing between the date line and the inside address according to the length of the letter.

17. The BEST title for the above passage would be
    A. Writing Office Letters
    B. Making Good First Impressions
    C. Judging Well-Typed Letters
    D. Good Placing and Spacing for Office Letters

17.____

18. According to the above passage, which of the following might be considered the way in which people very quickly judge the quality of work which has been typed? By
    A. measuring the margins to see if they are correct
    B. looking at the spacing and cleanliness of the typescript
    C. scanning the body of the letter for meaning
    D. reading the date line and address for errors

18.____

19. What, according to the above passage, would be definitely UNDESIRABLE as the average line length of a typed letter?
      A. 4"   B. 6"   C. 5"   D. 7"

20. According to the above passage, when the line length is kept standard, the secretary
      A. does not have to vary the spacing at all since this also is standard
      B. adjusts the spacing between the date line and inside address for different lengths of letters
      C. uses the longest line as a guidance for spacing between the date line and inside address
      D. varies the number of spaces between the lines

21. According to the above passage, side margins are MOST pleasing when they
      A. are even and somewhat smaller than the bottom margin
      B. are slightly wider than the bottom margin
      C. vary with the length of the letter
      D. are figured independently from the letterhead and the body of the letter

Questions 22-25.

DIRECTIONS: Questions 22 through 25 are to be answered SOLELY on the basis of the following passage.

Typed pages can reflect the simplicity of modern art in a machine age. Lightness and evenness can be achieved by proper layout and balance of typed lines and white space. Instead of solid, cramped masses of uneven, crowded typing, there should be a pleasing balance up and down as well as horizontal.

To have real balance, your page must have a center. The eyes see the center of the sheet slightly above the real center. This is the way both you and the reader see it. Try imagining a line down the center of the page that divides the paper in equal halves. On either side of your paper, white space and blocks of typing need to be similar in size and shape. Although left and right margins should be equal, top and bottom margins need not be as exact. It looks better to hold a bottom border wider than a top margin, so that your typing rests upon a cushion of white space. To add interest to the appearance of the page, try making one paragraph between one-half and two-thirds the size of an adjacent paragraph.

Thus, by taking full advantage of your typewriter, the pages that you type will not only be accurate but will also be attractive.

22. It can be inferred from the above passage that the basic importance of proper balancing on a typed page is that proper balancing
      A. makes a typed page a work of modern art
      B. provides exercise in proper positioning of a typewriter
      C. increases the amount of typed copy on the paper
      D. draws greater attention and interest to the page

23. A reader will tend to see the center of a typed page
    A. somewhat higher than the true center
    B. somewhat lower than the true center
    C. on either side of the true center
    D. about two-thirds of an inch above the true center

24. Which of the following suggestions is NOT given by the above passage?
    A. Bottom margins may be wider than top borders.
    B. Keep all paragraphs approximately the same size.
    C. Divide your page with an imaginary line down the middle.
    D. Side margins should be equalized.

25. Of the following, the BEST title for the above passage is
    A. Increasing the Accuracy of the Typed Page
    B. Determination of Margins for Typed Copy
    C. Layout and Balance of the Typed Page
    D. How to Take Full Advantage of the Typewriter

KEY (CORRECT ANSWERS)

1.	C		11.	B
2.	A		12.	A
3.	B		13.	B
4.	A		14.	B
5.	D		15.	A
6.	D		16.	B
7.	C		17.	D
8.	A		18.	B
9.	B		19.	D
10.	D		20.	B

21. A
22. D
23. A
24. B
25. C

TEST 3

DIRECTIONS: Each question or incomplete statement is followed by several suggested answers or completions. Select the one that BEST answers the question or completes the statement. *PRINT THE LETTER OF THE CORRECT ANSWER IN THE SPACE AT THE RIGHT.*

Questions 1-5.

DIRECTIONS: Questions 1 through 5 are to be answered SOLELY on the basis of the following passage.

    A written report is a communication of information from one person to another. It is an account of some matter especially investigated, however routine that matter may be. The ultimate basis of any good written report is facts, which become known through observation and verification. Good written reports may seem to be no more than general ideas and opinions. However, in such cases, the facts leading too these opinions were gathered, verified, and reported earlier, and the opinions are dependent upon these facts. Good style, proper form, and emphasis cannot make a good written report out of unreliable information and bad judgment; but on the other hand, solid investigation and brilliant thinking are not likely to become very useful until they are effectively communicated to others. If a person's work calls for written reports, then his work is often no better than his written reports.

1. Based on the information in the above passage, it can be concluded that opinions expressed in a report should be
   A. based on facts which are gathered and reported
   B. emphasized repeatedly when they result from a special investigation
   C. kept to a minimum
   D. separated from the body of the report

2. In the above passage, the one of the following which is mentioned as a way of establishing facts is
   A. authority
   B. reporting
   C. communication
   D. verification

3. According to the above passage, the characteristic shared by ALL written reports is that they are
   A. accounts of routine matters
   B. transmissions of information
   C. reliable and logical
   D. written in proper form

4. Which of the following conclusions can logically be drawn from the information given in the above passage?
   A. Brilliant thinking can make up for unreliable information in a report.
   B. One method of judging an individual's work is the quality of the written reports he is required to submit.
   C. Proper form and emphasis can make a good report out of unreliable information.
   D. Good written reports that seem to be no more than general ideas should be rewritten.

5. Which of the following suggested titles would be MOST appropriate for the above passage? 5._____
   A. Gathering and Organizing Facts
   B. Techniques of Observation
   C. Nature and Purpose of Reports
   D. Reports and Opinions: Differences and Similarities

Questions 6-8.

DIRECTIONS: Questions 6 through 8 are to be answered SOLELY on the basis of the following passage.

The most important unit of the mimeograph machine is a perforated metal drum over which is stretched a cloth ink pad. A reservoir inside the drum contains the ink which flows through the perforations and saturates the ink pad. To operate the machine, the operator first removes from the machine the protective sheet, which keeps the ink from drying while the machine is not in use. He then hooks the stencil face down on the drum, draws the stencil smoothly over the drum, and fastens the stencil at the bottom. The speed with which the drum turns determines the blackness of the copies printed. Slow turning gives heavy, black copies; fast turning gives light, clear-cut reproductions. If reproductions are run on other than porous paper, slip-sheeting is necessary to prevent smearing. Often, the printed copy fails to drop readily as it comes from the machine. This may be due to static electricity. To remedy this difficulty, the operator fastens a strip of tinsel from side to side near the impression roller so that the printed copy just touches the soft stems of the tinsel as it is ejected from the machine, thus grounding the static electricity to the frame of the machine.

6. According to the above passage, 6._____
   A. turning the drum fast produces light copies
   B. stencils should be placed face up on the drum
   C. ink pads should be changed daily
   D. slip-sheeting is necessary when porous paper is being used

7. According to the above passage, when a mimeograph machine is not in use, the 7._____
   A. ink should be drained from the drum
   B. ink pad should be removed
   C. machine should be covered with a protective sheet
   D. counter should be set at zero

8. According to the above passage, static electricity is grounded to the frame of the mimeograph machine by means of 8._____
   A. a slip-sheeting device
   B. a strip of tinsel
   C. an impression roller
   D. hooks located at the top of the drum

Questions 9-10.

DIRECTIONS: Questions 9 and 10 are to be answered SOLELY on the basis of the following passage.

The proofreading of material typed from copy is performed more accurately and more speedily when two persons perform this work as a team. The person who did not do the typing should read aloud the original copy while the person who did the typing should check the reading against the typed copy. The reader should speak very slowly and repeat the figures, using a different grouping of number when repeating the figures. For example, in reading 1967, the reader may say *one-nine-six-seven* on first reading the figure and *nineteen-sixty-seven* on repeating the figure. The reader should read all punctuation marks, taking nothing for granted. Since mistakes can occur anywhere, everything typed should be proofread. To avoid confusion, the proofreading team should use the standard proofreading marks, which are given in most dictionaries.

9. According to the above passage, the
    A. person who holds the typed copy is called the reader
    B. two members of a proofreading team should take turns in reading the typed copy aloud
    C. typed copy should be checked by the person who did the typing
    D. person who did not do the typing should read aloud from the typed copy

10. According to the above passage,
    A. it is unnecessary to read the period at the end of a sentence
    B. typographical errors should be noted on the original copy
    C. each person should develop his own set of proofreading marks
    D. figures should be read twice

Questions 11-16.

DIRECTIONS: Questions 11 through 16 are to be answered SOLELY on the basis of the following passage.

Basic to every office is the need for proper lighting. Inadequate lighting is a familiar cause of fatigue and serves to create a somewhat dismal atmosphere in the office. One requirement of proper lighting is that it be of an appropriate intensity. Intensity is measured in foot-candles. According to the Illuminating Engineering Society of New York, for casual seeing tasks such as in reception rooms, inactive file rooms, and other service areas, it is recommending that the amount of light be 30 foot-candle. For ordinary seeing tasks such as reading, work in active file rooms, and in mailrooms, the recommended lighting is 100 foot-candles. For very difficult seeing tasks such as accounting, transcribing, and business machine use, the recommended lighting is 150 foot-candles.

Lighting intensity is only one requirement. Shadows and glare are to be avoided. For example, the larger the proportion of a ceiling filled with lighting units, the more glare-free and comfortable the lighting will be. Natural lighting from window is not too dependable because on dark wintry days, windows yield little usable light, and on sunny afternoons, the glare from windows may be very distracting. Desks should not face the windows. Finally, the main lighting source ought to be overhead and to the left of the user.

11. According to the above passage, insufficient light in the office may cause   11.____
    A. glare   B. tiredness   C. shadows   D. distraction

12. Based on the above passage, which of the following must be considered   12.____
    when planning lighting arrangements? The
    A. amount of natural light present
    B. amount of work to be done
    C. level of difficulty of work to be done
    D. type of activity to be carried out

13. It can be inferred from the above passage that a well-coordinated lighting   13.____
    scheme is LIKELY to result in
    A. greater employee productivity   B. elimination of light reflection
    C. lower lighting cost   D. more use of natural light

14. Of the following, the BEST title for the above passage is   14.____
    A. Characteristics of Light
    B. Light Measurement Devices
    C. Factors to Consider When Planning Lighting Systems
    D. comfort vs. Cost When Devising Lighting Arrangements

15. According to the above passage, a foot-candle is a measurement of the   15.____
    A. number of bulbs used
    B. strength of the light
    C. contrast between glare and shadow
    D. proportion of the ceiling filled with lighting units

16. According to the above passage, the number of foot-candles of light that   16.____
    would be needed to copy figures onto a payroll is _____ foot-candles.
    A. less than 30   B. 100   C. 30   D. 140

Questions 17-23.

DIRECTIONS: Questions 17 through 23 are to be answered SOLELY on the basis of the following passage.

FEE SCHEDULE

1. A candidate for any baccalaureate degree is not required to pay tuition fees for undergraduate courses until he exceeds 128 credits. Candidates exceeding 128 credits in undergraduate courses are charged at the rate of $100 a credit for each credit of undergraduate course work in excess of 128. Candidates for a baccalaureate degree who are taking graduate courses must pay the same fee as any other student taking graduate courses.

B. Non-degree students and college graduates are charged tuition fees for courses, whether undergraduate or graduate, at the rate of $180 a credit. For such students, there is an additional charge of $150 for each class hour per week in excess of the number of course credits. For example, if a three-credit course meets five hours a week, there is an additional charge for the extra two hours. Graduate courses are shown with a (G) before the course number.

C. All students are required to pay the laboratory fees indicated after the number of credits given for that course.

D. All students must pay a $250 general fee each semester.

E. Candidates for a baccalaureate degree are charged a $150 medical insurance fee for each semester. All other students are charged a $100 medical insurance fee each semester.

17. Miss Burton is not a candidate for a degree. She registers for the following courses in the spring semester: Economics 12, 4 hours a week, 3 credits; History (G 23, 4 hours a week, 3 credits; English 1, 2 hours a week, 2 credits. The TOTAL amount in fees that Miss Burton must pay is
    A. less than $2,000
    B. at least $2,000 but less than $2,100
    C. at least $2,100 but less than $2,200
    D. $2,200 or over

18. Miss Gray is not a candidate for a degree. She registers for the following courses in the fall semester: History 3, 3 hours a week, 3 credits; English 5, 3 hours a week, 2 credits; Physics 5, 6 hours a week, 3 credits, laboratory fee $60; Mathematics 7, 4 hours a week, 3 credits. The TOTAL amount in fees that Miss Gray must pay is
    A. less than $3,150
    B. at least $3,150 but less than $3,250
    C. at least $3,250 but less than $3,350
    D. $3,350 or over

19. Mr. Wall is a candidate for the Bachelor of Arts degree and has completed 126 credits. He registers for the following courses in the spring semester, his final semester at college; French 4, 3 hours a week, 3 credits; Physics (G) 15, 6 hours a week, 3 credits, laboratory fee $80; History (G) 33, 4 hours a week, 3 credits. The TOTAL amount in fees that this candidate must pay is
    A. less than $2,100
    B. at least $2,100 but less than $2,300
    C. at least $2,300 but less than $2,500
    D. $2,500

6 (#3)

20. Mr. Tindall, a candidate for the B.A. degree, has completed 122 credits of undergraduate courses. He registers for the following courses in his final semester: English 31, 3 hours a week, 3 credits; Philosophy 12, 4 hours a week, 4 credits; Anthropology 15, 3 hours a week, 3 credits; Economics (G) 68, 3 hours a week, 3 credits.
    The TOTAL amount in fees that Mr. Tindall must pay in his final semester is
    A. less than $1,200
    B. at least $1,200 but less than $1,400
    C. at least $1,400 but less than $1,600
    D. $1,600

    20.____

21. Mr. Cantrell, who was graduated from the college a year ago, registers for graduate courses in the fall semester. Each course for which he register carries the same number of credits as the number of hours a week it meets. If he pays a total of $1,530, including a $100 laboratory fee, the number of credits for which he is registered is
    A. 4   B. 5   C. 6   D. 7

    21.____

22. Miss Jayson, who is not a candidate for a degree, has registered for several courses including a lecture course in History. She withdraws from the course in History for which she had paid the required course fee of $690.
    The number of hours that this course is scheduled to meet is
    A. 4   B. 5   C. 2   D. 3

    22.____

23. Mr. Van Arsdale, a graduate of a college in Iowa, registers for the following courses in one semester: Chemistry 35, 5 hours a week, 3 credits; Biology 14, 4 hours a week, 3 credits, laboratory fee $150; Mathematics (G) 179, 3 hours a week, 3 credits.
    The TOTAL amount in fees that Mr. Van Arsdale must pay is
    A. less than $2,400
    B. at least $2,400 but less than $2,500
    C. at least $2,500 but less than $2,600
    D. at least $2,600 or over

    23.____

Questions 24-25.

DIRECTIONS: Questions 24 and 25 are to be answered SOLELY on the basis of the following passage.

A duplex envelope is an envelope composed of two sections securely fastened together so that they become one mailing piece. This type of envelope makes it possible for a first class letter to be delivered simultaneously with third or fourth class matter and yet not require payment of the much higher first class postage rate on the entire mailing. First class postage is paid only on the letter which goes in the small compartment, third or fourth class postage being paid on the contents of the larger compartment. The larger compartment generally has an ungummed flap or clasp for sealing. The first class or smaller compartment has a gummed flap for sealing. Postal regulations require that the exact amount of postage applicable to each compartment be separately attached to it.

24. On the basis of the above passage, it is MOST accurate to state that
    A. the smaller compartment is placed inside the larger compartment before mailing
    B. the two compartments may be detached and mailed separately
    C. two classes of mailing matter may be mailed as a unit at two different postage rates
    D. the more expensive postage rate is paid on the matter in the larger compartment

25. When a duplex envelope is used, the
    A. first class compartment may be sealed with a clasp
    B. correct amount of postage must be placed on each compartment
    C. compartment containing third or fourth class mail requires a gummed flap for sealing
    D. full amount of postage for both compartments may be placed on the larger compartment

KEY (CORRECT ANSWERS)

1.	A	11.	C
2.	D	12.	D
3.	B	13.	A
4.	B	14.	C
5.	C	15.	B
6.	A	16.	D
7.	C	17.	B
8.	B	18.	A
9.	C	19.	B
10.	D	20.	B

21.	C
22.	A
23.	C
24.	C
25.	B

PREPARING WRITTEN MATERIALS
EXAMINATION SECTION
TEST 1

DIRECTIONS: Each question consists of a sentence which may be classified appropriately under one of the following four categories:
- A. Incorrect because of faulty grammar or sentence structure;
- B. Incorrect because of faulty punctuation;
- C. Incorrect because of faulty capitalization;
- D. Correct

Examine each sentence carefully. Then, in the space at the right, indicate the letter preceding the category which is the BEST of the four suggested above. Each incorrect sentence contains only one type of error. Consider a sentence correct if it contains no errors, although there may be other correct ways of expressing the same thought.

1. All the employees, in this office, are over twenty-one years old.   1.____

2. Neither the clerk nor the stenographer was able to explain what had happened.   2.____

3. Mr. Johnson did not know who he would assign to type the order.   3.____

4. Mr. Marshall called her to report for work on Saturday.   4.____

5. He might of arrived on time if the train has not been delayed.   5.____

6. Some employees on the other hand, are required to fill out these forms every month.   6.____

7. The supervisor issued special instructions to his subordinates to prevent their making errors.   7.____

8. Our supervisor Mr. Williams, expects to be promoted in about two weeks.   8.____

9. We were informed that prof. Morgan would attend the conference.   9.____

10. The clerks were assigned to the old building; the stenographers, to the new building.   10.____

11. The supervisor asked Mr. Smith and I to complete the work as quickly as possible.   11.____

12. He said, that before an employee can be permitted to leave, the report must be finished.   12.____

13. A calculator, in addition to the three computers, are needed in the   13.____
    new office.

14. Having made many errs in her work, the supervisor asked the typist to be   14.____
    more careful.

15. "If you are given an assignment," he said, "you should begin work on it as 15.____
    quickly as possible."

16. All the clerks, including those who have been appointed recently are required 16.____
    to work on the new assignment.

17. The office manager asked each employee to work one Saturday a month.   17.____

18. Neither Mr. Smith nor Mr. Jones was able to finish his assignment on time. 18.___

19. The task of filing these cards is to be divided equally between you and he. 19.____

20. He is an employee whom we consider to be efficient.   20.____

21. I believe that the new employees are not as punctual as us.   21.____

22. The employees, working in this office, are to be congratulated for their work. 22.____

23. The delay in preparing the report was caused, in his opinion, by the lack of 23.____
    proper supervision and coordination.

24. John Jones accidentally pushed the wrong button and then all the lights   24.____
    went out.

25. The investigator ought to of had the witness sign the statement.   25.____

KEY (CORRECT ANSWERS)

1.	B	11.	A
2.	D	12.	B
3.	A	13.	A
4.	C	14.	A
5.	A	15.	D
6.	B	16.	B
7.	D	17.	C
8.	B	18.	D
9.	C	19.	A
10.	D	20.	D

21. A
22. B
23. D
24. D
25. A

TEST 2

Questions 1-10.

DIRECTIONS: Each of the following sentences may be classified under one of the following four options:
- A. Faulty; contains an error in grammar only
- B. Faulty; contains an error in spelling only
- C. Faulty; contains an error in grammar and an error in spelling
- D. Correct; contains no error in grammar or in spelling

Examine each sentence carefully to determine under which of the above four options it is BEST classified. Then, in the space at the right, write the letter preceding the option which is the best of the four listed above.

1. A recognized principle of good management is that an assignment should be given to whomever is best qualified to carry it out. 1.____

2. He considered it a privilege to be allowed to review and summarize the technical reports issued annually by your agency. 2.____

3. Because the warehouse was in an inaccessible location, deliveries of electric fixtures from the warehouse were made only in large lots. 3.____

4. Having requisitioned the office supplies, Miss Brown returned to her desk and resumed the computation of petty cash disbursements. 4.____

5. One of the advantages of this chemical solution is that records treated with it are not inflamable. 5.____

6. The complaint of this employee, in addition to the complaints of the other employees, were submitted to the grievance committee. 6.____

7. A study of the duties and responsibilities of each of the various categories of employees was conducted by an unprejudiced classification analyst. 7.____

8. Ties of friendship with this subordinate compels him to withold the censure that the subordinate deserves. 8.____

9. Neither of the agencies are affected by the decision to institute a program for rehabilitating physically handi-caped men and women. 9.____

10. The chairman stated that the argument between you and he was creating an intolerable situation. 10.____

Questions 11-25.

DIRECTIONS: Each of the following sentences may be classified under one of the following four options:
  A. Correct
  B. Sentence contains an error in spelling
  C. Sentence contains an error in grammar
  D. Sentence contains errors in both grammar and spelling.

11. He reported that he had had a really good time during his vacation although the farm was located in a very inaccessible portion of the country. 11.____

12. It looks to me like he has been fasinated by that beautiful painting. 12.____

13. We have permitted these kind of pencils to accumulate on our shelves, knowing we can sell them at a profit of five cents apiece any time we choose. 13.____

14. Believing that you will want an unexagerated estimate of the amount of business we can expect, I have made every effort to secure accurate figures. 14.____

15. Each and every man, woman and child in that untrammeled wilderness carry guns for protection against the wild animals. 15.____

16. Although this process is different than the one to which he is accustomed, a good chemist will have no trouble. 16.____

17. Insensible to the fuming and fretting going on about him, the engineer continued to drive the mammoth dynamo to its utmost capacity. 17.____

18. Everyone had studied his lesson carefully and was consequently well prepared when the instructor began to discuss the fourth dimention. 18.____

19. I learned Johnny six new arithmetic problems this afternoon. 19.____

20. Athletics is urged by our most prominent citizens as the pursuit which will enable the younger generation to achieve that ideal of education, a sound mind in a sound body. 20.____

21. He did not see whoever was at the door very clearly but thinks it was the city tax appraiser. 21.____

22. He could not scarsely believe that his theories had been substantiated in this convincing fashion. 22.____

23. Although you have displayed great ingenuity in carrying out your assignments, the choice for the position still lies among Brown and Smith. 23.____

24. If they had have pleaded at the time that Smith was an accessory to the crime, it would have lessened the punishment. 24.____

25. It has proven indispensible in his compilation of the facts in the matter. 25.____

KEY (CORRECT ANSWERS)

1.	A		11.	A
2.	D		12.	D
3.	B		13.	C
4.	D		14.	B
5.	B		15.	D
6.	A		16.	C
7.	D		17.	A
8.	C		18.	B
9.	C		19.	C
10.	A		20.	A

21. B
22. D
23. C
24. D
25. B

TEST 3

Questions 1-5.

DIRECTIONS: Questions 1 through 5 consist of sentences which may or may not contain errors in grammar or spelling or both. Sentences which do not contain errors in grammar or spelling or both are to be considered correct, even though there may be other correct ways of expressing the same thought. Examine each sentence carefully. Then, in the space at the right, write the letter of the answer which is the BEST of those suggested below.
    A. If the sentence is correct
    B. If the sentence contains an error in spelling
    C. If the sentence contains an error in grammar
    D. If the sentence contains errors in both grammar and spelling.

1. Brown is doing fine although the work is irrevelant to his training.   1.____

2. The conference of sales managers voted to set its adjournment at one o'clock in order to give those present an opportunity to get rid of all merchandise.   2.____

3. He decided that in view of what had taken place at the hotel that he ought to stay and thank the benificent stranger who had rescued him from an embarassing situation.   3.____

4. Since you object to me criticizing your letter, I have no alternative but to consider you a mercenary scoundrel.   4.____

5. I rushed home ahead of schedule so that you will leave me go to the picnic with Mary.   5.____

Questions 6-15.

DIRECTIONS: Some of the following sentences contain an error in spelling, word usage, or sentence structure, or punctuation. Some sentences are correct as they stand although there may be other correct ways of expressing the same thought. All incorrect sentences contain only one error. Mark your answer to each question in the space at the right as follows:
    A. If the sentence has an error in spelling
    B. If the sentence has an error in punctuation or capitalization
    C. If the sentence has an error in word usage or sentence structure
    D. If the sentence is correct

6. Because the chairman failed to keep the participants from wandering off into irrelevant discussions, it was impossible to reach a consensus before the meeting was adjourned.   6.____

7. Certain employers have an unwritten rule that any applicant, who is over 55 years of age, is automatically excluded from consideration for any position whatsoever.   7.____

8. If the proposal to build schools in some new apartment buildings were to be accepted by the builders, one of the advantages that could be expected to result would be better communication between teachers and parents of schoolchildren.   8.____

9. In this instance, the manufacturer's violation of the law against deseptive packaging was discernible only to an experienced inspector.   9.____

10. The tenants' anger stemmed from the president's going to Washington to testify without consulting them first.   10.____

11. Did the president of this eminent banking company say; "We intend to hire and train a number of these disadvantaged youths?"   11.____

12. In addition, today's confidential secretary must be knowledgable in many different areas: for example, she must know modern techniques for making travel arrangements for the executive.   12.____

13. To avoid further disruption of work in the offices, the protesters were forbidden from entering the building unless they had special passes.   13.____

14. A valuable secondary result of our training conferences is the opportunities afforded for management to observe the reactions of the participants.   14.____

15. Of the two proposals submitted by the committee, the first one is the best.   15.____

Questions 16-25.

DIRECTIONS: Each of the following sentences may be classified MOST appropriately under one of the following three categories:
A. Faulty because of incorrect grammar
B. Faulty because of incorrect punctuation
C. Correct

Examine each sentence. Then, print the capital letter preceding the BEST choice of the three suggested above. All incorrect sentences contain only one type of error. Consider a sentence correct if it contains none of the types of errors mentioned, even though there may be other ways of expressing the same thought.

16. He sent the notice to the clerk who you hired yesterday.   16.____

17. It must be admitted, however that you were not informed of this change.   17.____

18. Only the employees who have served in this grade for at least two years are eligible for promotion.   18.____

19. The work was divided equally between she and Mary.   19.____

20. He thought that you were not available at that time. 20._____

21. When the messenger returns; please give him this package. 21._____

22. The new secretary prepared, typed, addressed, and delivered, the notices. 22._____

23. Walking into the room, his desk can be seen at the rear. 23._____

24. Although John has worked here longer than she, he produces a smaller amount of work. 24._____

25. She said she could of typed this report yesterday. 25._____

KEY (CORRECT ANSWERS)

1. D 11. B
2. A 12. A
3. D 13. C
4. C 14. D
5. C 15. C

6. A 16. A
7. B 17. B
8. D 18. C
9. A 19. A
10. D 20. C

21. B
22. B
23. A
24. C
25. A

TEST 4

Questions 1-5.

DIRECTIONS: Each of the following sentences may be classified MOST appropriately under one of the following three categories:
- A. Faulty because of incorrect grammar
- B. Faulty because of incorrect punctuation
- C. Correct

Examine each sentence. Then, print the capital letter preceding the BEST choice of the three suggested above. All incorrect sentences contain only one type of error. Consider a sentence correct if it contains none of the types of errors mentioned, even though there may be other ways of expressing the same thought.

1. Neither one of these procedures are adequate for the efficient performance of this task.   1.____

2. The keyboard is the tool of the typist; the cash register, the tool of the cashier.   2.____

3. "The assignment must be completed as soon as possible" said the supervisor.   3.____

4. As you know, office handbooks are issued to all new employees.   4.____

5. Writing a speech is sometimes easier than to deliver it before an audience.   5.____

Questions 6-15.

DIRECTIONS: Each statement given in Questions 6 through 15 contains one of the faults of English usage listed below. For each, choose from the options listed the MAJOR fault contained.
- A. The statement is not a complete sentence.
- B. The statement contains a word or phrase that is redundant.
- C. The statement contains a long, less commonly used word when a shorter, more direct word would be acceptable.
- D. The statement contains a colloquial expression that normally is avoided in business writing.

6. The fact that this activity will afford an opportunity to meet your group.   6.____

7. Do you think that the two groups can join together for next month's meeting?   7.____

8. This is one of the most exciting new innovations to be introduced into our college.   8.____

9. We expect to consummate the agenda before the meeting ends tomorrow at noon. 9._____

10. While this seminar room is small in size, we think we can use it. 10._____

11. Do you think you can make a modification in the date of the Budget Committee meeting? 11._____

12. We are cognizant of the problem but we think we can ameliorate the situation. 12._____

13. Shall I call you around three on the day I arrive in the City? 13._____

14. Until such time that we know precisely that the students will be present. 14._____

15. The consensus of opinion of all the members present is reported in the minutes. 15._____

Questions 16-25.

DIRECTIONS: For each of Questions 16 through 25, select from the options given below the MOST applicable choice.
    A. The sentence is correct.
    B. The sentence contains a spelling error only.
    C. The sentence contains an English grammar error only.
    D. The sentence contains both a spelling error and an English grammar error.

16. Every person in the group is going to do his share. 16._____

17. The man who we selected is new to this University. 17._____

18. She is the older of the four secretaries on the two staffs that are to be combined. 18._____

19. The decision has to be made between him and I. 19._____

20. One of the volunteers are too young for his complicated task, don't you think? 20._____

21. I think your idea is splindid and it will improve this report considerably. 21._____

22. Do you think this is an exagerated account of the behavior you and me observed this morning? 22._____

23. Our supervisor has a clear idea of excelence. 23._____

24. How many occurences were verified by the observers? 24._____

25. We must complete the typing of the draft of the questionaire by noon tomorrow. 25.____

KEY (CORRECT ANSWERS)

1. A
2. C
3. B
4. C
5. A

6. A
7. B
8. B
9. C
10. B

11. C
12. C
13. D
14. A
15. B

16. A
17. C
18. C
19. C
20. D

21. B
22. D
23. B
24. B
25. B

PRINCIPLES AND PRACTICES, OF ADMINISTRATION, SUPERVISION AND MANAGEMENT

TABLE OF CONTENTS

	Page
GENERAL ADMINISTRATION	1
SEVEN BASIC FUNCTIONS OF THE SUPERVISOR	2
I. Planning	2
II. Organizing	3
III. Staffing	3
IV. Directing	3
V. Coordinating	3
VI. Reporting	3
VII. Budgeting	3
PLANNING TO MEET MANAGEMENT GOALS	4
I. What is Planning	4
II. Who Should Make Plans	4
III. What are the Results of Poor Planning	4
IV. Principles of Planning	4
MANAGEMENT PRINCIPLES	5
I. Management	5
II. Management Principles	5
III. Organization Structure	6
ORGANIZATION	8
I. Unity of Command	8
II. Span of Control	8
III. Uniformity of Assignment	9
IV. Assignment of Responsibility and Delegation of Authority	9
PRINCIPLES OF ORGANIZATION	9
I. Definition	9
II. Purpose of Organization	9
III. Basic Considerations in Organizational Planning	9
IV. Bases for Organization	10
V. Assignment of Functions	10
VI. Delegation of Authority and Responsibility	10
VII. Employee Relationships	11

DELEGATING		11
I.	WHAT IS DELEGATING:	11
II.	TO WHOM TO DELEGATE	11
REPORTS		12
I.	DEFINITION	12
II.	PURPOSE	12
III.	TYPES	12
IV.	FACTORS TO CONSIDER BEFORE WRITING REPORT	12
V.	PREPARATORY STEPS	12
VI.	OUTLINE FOR A RECOMMENDATION REPORT	12
MANAGEMENT CONTROLS		13
I.	Control	13
II.	Basis for Control	13
III.	Policy	13
IV.	Procedure	14
V.	Basis of Control	14
FRAMEWORK OF MANAGEMENT		14
I.	Elements	14
II.	Manager's Responsibility	15
III.	Control Techniques	16
IV.	Where Forecasts Fit	16
PROBLEM SOLVING		16
I.	Identify the Problem	16
II.	Gather Data	17
III.	List Possible Solutions	17
IV.	Test Possible Solutions	18
V.	Select the Best Solution	18
VI.	Put the Solution into Actual Practice	19
COMMUNICATION		19
I.	What is Communication?	19
II.	Why is Communication Needed?	19
III.	How is Communication Achieved?	20
IV.	Why Does Communication Fail?	21
V.	How to Improve Communication	21
VI.	How to Determine If You Are Getting Across	21
VII.	The Key Attitude	22
HOW ORDERS AND INSTRUCTIONS SHOULD BE GIVEN		22
I.	Characteristics of Good Orders and Instructions	22
FUNCTIONS OF A DEPARTMENT PERSONNEL OFFICE		23

SUPERVISION		23
I.	Leadership	23
	A. The Authoritarian Approach	23
	B. The Laissez-Faire Approach	24
	C. The Democratic Approach	24
II.	Nine Points of Contrast Between Boss and Leader	25
EMPLOYEE MORALE		25
I.	Some Ways to Develop and Maintain Good Employee Morale	25
II.	Some Indicators of Good Morale	26
MOTIVATION		26
EMPLOYEE PARTICIPATION		27
I.	WHAT IS PARTICIPATION	27
II.	WHY IS IT IMPORTANT?	27
III.	HOW MAY SUPERVISORS OBTAIN IT?	28
STEPS IN HANDLING A GRIEVANCE		28
DISCIPLINE		29
I.	THE DISCIPLINARY INTERVIEW	29
II.	PLANNING THE INTERVIEW	29
III.	CONDUCTING THE INTERVIEW	30

PRINCIPLES AND PRACTICES, OF ADMINISTRATION, SUPERVISION AND MANAGEMENT

Most people are inclined to think of administration as something that only a few persons are responsible for in a large organization. Perhaps this is true if you are thinking of Administration with a capital A, but administration with a lower case a is a responsibility of supervisors at all levels each working day.

All of us feel we are pretty good supervisors and that we do a good job of administering the workings of our agency. By and large, this is true, but every so often it is good to check up on ourselves. Checklists appear from time to time in various publications which psychologists say tell whether or not a person will make a good wife, husband, doctor, lawyer, or supervisor.

The following questions are an excellent checklist to test yourself as a supervisor and administrator.

Remember, Administration gives direction and points the way but administration carries the ideas to fruition. Each is dependent on the other for its success. Remember, too, that no unit is too small for these departmental functions to be carried out. These statements apply equally as well to the Chief Librarian as to the Department Head with but one or two persons to supervise.

GENERAL ADMINISTRATION: General Responsibilities of Supervisors

1. Have I prepared written statements of functions, activities, and duties for my organizational unit?

2. Have I prepared procedural guides for operating activities?

3. Have I established clearly in writing, lines of authority and responsibility for my organizational unit?

4. Do I make recommendations for improvements in organization, policies, administrative and operating routines and procedures, including simplification of work and elimination of non-essential operations?

5. Have I designated and trained an understudy to function in my absence?

6. Do I supervise and train personnel within the unit to effectively perform their assignments?

7. Do I assign personnel and distribute work on such a basis as to carry out the organizational unit's assignment or mission in the most effective and efficient manner?

8. Have I established administrative controls by:

    a. Fixing responsibility and accountability on all supervisors under my direction for the proper performance of their functions and duties.

b. Preparations and submitting periodic work load and progress reports covering the operations of the unit to my immediate superior.

c. Analysis and evaluation of such reports received from subordinate units.

d. Submission of significant developments and problems arising within the organizational unit to my immediate superior.

e. Conducting conferences, inspections, etc., as to the status and efficiency of unit operations.

9. Do I maintain an adequate and competent working force?

10. Have I fostered good employee-department relations, seeing that established rules, regulations, and instructions are being carried out properly?

11. Do I collaborate and consult with other organizational units performing related functions to insure harmonious and efficient working relationships?

12. Do I maintain liaison through prescribed channels with city departments and other governmental agencies concerned with the activities of the unit?

13. Do I maintain contact with and keep abreast of the latest developments and techniques of administration (professional societies, groups, periodicals, etc.) as to their applicability to the activities of the unit?

14. Do I communicate with superiors and subordinates through prescribed organizational channels?

15. Do I notify superiors and subordinates in instances where bypassing is necessary as soon thereafter as practicable?

16. Do I keep my superior informed of significant developments and problems?

SEVEN BASIC FUNCTIONS OF THE SUPERVISOR

I. PLANNING
This means working out goals and means to obtain goals. <u>What</u> needs to be done, <u>who</u> will do it, <u>how</u>, <u>when</u>, and <u>where</u> it is to be done.

SEVEN STEPS IN PLANNING

A. Define job or problem clearly.
B. Consider priority of job.
C. Consider time-limit—starting and completing.
D. Consider minimum distraction to, or interference with, other activities.
E. Consider and provide for contingencies—possible emergencies.
F. Break job down into components.

G. Consider the 5 W's and H:
   WHY……….is it necessary to do the job? (Is the purpose clearly defined?)
   WHAT……..needs to be done to accomplish the defined purpose?
   ……….is needed to do the job? (Money, materials, etc.)
   WHO……….is needed to do the job?
   ……….will have responsibilities?
   WHERE……is the work to be done?
   WHEN……..is the job to begin and end? (Schedules, etc.)
   HOW……….is the job to bed done? (Methods, controls, records, etc.)

II. ORGANIZING

This means dividing up the work, establishing clear lines of responsibility and authority and coordinating efforts to get the job done.

III. STAFFING

The whole personnel function of bringing in and training staff, getting the right man and fitting him to the right job—the job to which he is best suited.

In the normal situation, the supervisor's responsibility regarding staffing normally includes providing accurate job descriptions, that is, duties of the jobs, requirements, education and experience, skills, physical, etc.; assigning the work for maximum use of skills; and proper utilization of the probationary period to weed out unsatisfactory employees.

IV. DIRECTING

Providing the necessary leadership to the group supervised. Important work gets done to the supervisor's satisfaction.

V. COORDINATING

The all-important duty of inter-relating the various parts of the work.
The supervisor is also responsible for controlling the coordinated activities. This means measuring performance according to a time schedule and setting quotas to see that the goals previously set are being reached. Reports from workers should be analyzed, evaluated, and made part of all future plans.

VI. REPORTING

This means proper and effective communication to your superiors, subordinates, and your peers (in definition of the job of the supervisor). Reports should be read and information contained therein should be used, not be filed away and forgotten. Reports should be written in such a way that the desired action recommended by the report is forthcoming.

VII. BUDGETING
This means controlling current costs and forecasting future costs. This forecast is based on past experience, future plans and programs, as well as current costs.

You will note that these seven functions can fall under three topics:

Planning) Make a plan
Organizing)

Staffing)
Directing) Get things done
Controlling)

Reporting) Watch it work
Budgeting)

PLANNING TO MEET MANAGEMENT GOALS

I. WHAT IS PLANNING?

    A. Thinking a job through before new work is done to determine the best way to do it
    B. A method of doing something
    C. Ways and means for achieving set goals
    D. A means of enabling a supervisor to deliver with a minimum of effort, all details involved in coordinating his work

II. WHO SHOULD MAKE PLANS?

Everybody!
All levels of supervision must plan work. (Top management, heads of divisions or bureaus, first line supervisors, and individual employees.) The higher the level, the more planning required.

III. WHAT ARE THE RESULTS OF POOR PLANNING?

    A. Failure to meet deadline
    B. Low employee morale
    C. Lack of job coordination
    D. Overtime is frequently necessary
    E. Excessive cost, waste of material and manhours

IV. PRINCIPLES OF PLANNING

    A. Getting a clear picture of your objectives. What exactly are you trying to accomplish?
    B. Plan the whole job, then the parts, in proper sequence.
    C. Delegate the planning of details to those responsible for executing them.
    D. Make your plan flexible.
    E. Coordinate your plan with the plans of others so that the work may be processed with a minimum of delay.
    F. Sell your plan before you execute it.
    G. Sell your plan to your superior, subordinate, in order to gain maximum participation and coordination.
    H. Your plan should take precedence. Use knowledge and skills that others have brought to a similar job.
    I. Your plan should take account of future contingencies; allow for future expansion.
    J. Plans should include minor details. Leave nothing to chance that can be anticipated.
    K. Your plan should be simple and provide standards and controls. Establish quality and quantity standards and set a standard method of doing the job. The controls will indicate whether the job is proceeding according to plan.
    L. Consider possible bottlenecks, breakdowns, or other difficulties that are likely to arise.

V. Q. WHAT ARE THE YARDSTICKS BY WHICH PLANNING SHOULD BE MEASURED?
    A. Any plan should:
       —Clearly state a definite course of action to be followed and goal to be achieved, with consideration for emergencies.
       — Be realistic and practical.
       — State what's to be done, when it's to be done, where, how, and by whom.
       — Establish the most efficient sequence of operating steps so that more is accomplished in less time, with the least effort, and with the best quality results.
       — Assure meeting deliveries without delays.
       — Establish the standard by which performance is to be judged.

    Q. WHAT KINDS OF PLANS DOES EFFECTIVE SUPERVISION REQUIRE?
    A. Plans should cover such factors as:
       — Manpower: right number of properly trained employees on the job
       — Materials: adequate supply of the right materials and supplies
       — Machines: full utilization of machines and equipment, with proper maintenance
       — Methods: most efficient handling of operations
       — Deliveries: making deliveries on time
       — Tools: sufficient well-conditioned tools
       — Layout: most effective use of space
       — Reports: maintaining proper records and reports
       — Supervision: planning work for employees and organizing supervisor's own time

MANAGEMENT PRINCIPLES

I. MANAGEMENT
    Q. What do we mean by management?
    A. Getting work done through others.

    Management could also be defined as planning, directing, and controlling the operations of a bureau or division so that all factors will function properly and all persons cooperate efficiently for a common objective.

II. MANAGEMENT PRINCIPLES

    A. There should be a hierarchy—wherein authority and responsibility run upward and downward through several levels—with a broad base at the bottom and a single head at the top.

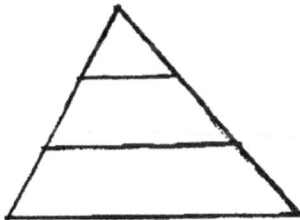

    B. Each and every unit or person in the organization should be answerable ultimately to the manager at the apex. In other words, *The buck stops here!*

C. Every necessary function involved in the bureau's objectives is assigned to a unit in that bureau.

D. Responsibilities assigned to a unit are specifically clear-cut and understood.

E. Consistent methods of organizational structure should be applied at each level of the organization.

F. Each member of the bureau from top to bottom knows: to whom he reports and who reports to him.

G. No member of one bureau reports to more than one supervisor. No dual functions.

H. Responsibility for a function is matched by authority necessary to perform that function. Weight of authority.

I. Individuals or units reporting to a supervisor do not exceed the number which can be feasibly and effectively coordinated and directed. Concept of *span of control*.

J. Channels of command (management) are not violated by staff units, although there should be staff services to facilitate and coordinate management functions.

K. Authority and responsibility should be decentralized to units and individuals who are responsible for the actual performance of operations.
Welfare – down to Welfare Centers
Hospitals – down to local hospitals

L. Management should exercise control through attention to policy problems of exceptional performance, rather than through review of routine actions of subordinates.

M. Organizations should never be permitted to grow so elaborate as to hinder work accomplishments.

III. ORGANIZATION STRUCTURE

Types of Organizations
The purest form is a leader and a few followers, such as:

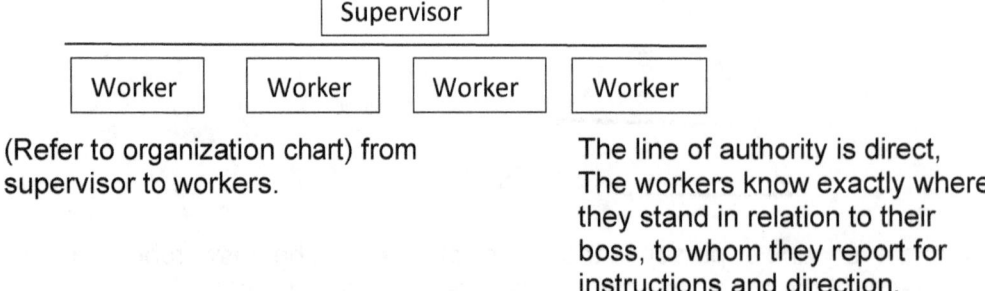

(Refer to organization chart) from supervisor to workers.

The line of authority is direct, The workers know exactly where they stand in relation to their boss, to whom they report for instructions and direction.

Unfortunately, in our present complex society, few organizations are similar to this example of a pure line organization. In this era of specialization, other people are often needed in the simplest of organizations. These specialists are known as staff. The sole purpose for their existence (staff) is to assist, advise, suggest, help or counsel line organizations. Staff has no authority to direct line people—nor do they give them direct instructions.

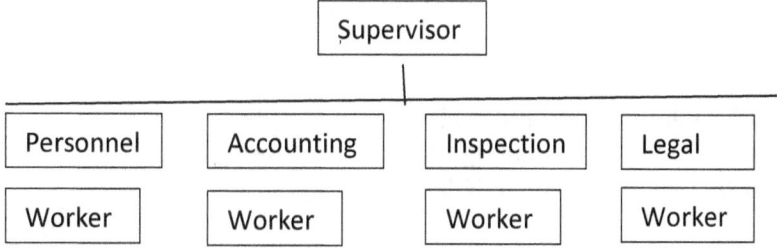

Line Functions
1. Directs
2. Orders
3. Responsibility for carrying out activities from beginning to end
4. Follows chain of command
5. Is identified with what it does
6. Decides when and how to use staff advice
7. Line executes

Staff Functions
1. Advises
2. Persuades and sells
3. Staff studies, reports, recommends but does not carry out
4. May advise across department lines
5. May find its ideas identified with others
6. Has to persuade line to want its advice
7. Staff: Conducts studies and research. Provides advice and instructions in technical matters. Serves as technical specialist to render specific services.

Types and Functions of Organization Charts
An organization chart is a picture of the arrangement and inter-relationship of the subdivisions of an organization.

A. Types of Charts:
   1. Structural: basic relationships only
   2. Functional: includes functions or duties
   3. Personnel: positions, salaries, status, etc.
   4. Process Chart: work performed
   5. Gantt Chart: actual performance against planned
   5. Flow Chart: flow and distribution of work

B. Functions of Charts:
   1. Assist in management planning and control
   2. Indicate duplication of functions
   3. Indicate incorrect stressing of functions
   4. Indicate neglect of important functions
   5. Correct unclear authority
   6. Establish proper span of control

C. Limitations of Charts:
   1. Seldom maintained on current basis
   2. Chart is oversimplified
   3. Human factors cannot adequately be charted

D. Organization Charts should be:
   1. Simple
   2. Symmetrical
   3. Indicate authority
   4. Line and staff relationship differentiated
   5. Chart should be dated and bear signature of approving officer
   6. Chart should be displayed, not hidden

ORGANIZATION

There are four basic principles of organization:
1. Unity of command
2. Span of control
3. Uniformity of assignment
4. Assignment of responsibility and delegation of authority

I. UNITY OF COMMAND

Unity of command means that each person in the organization should receive orders from one, and only one, supervisor. When a person has to take orders from two or more people, (a) the orders may be in conflict and the employee is upset because he does not know which he should obey, or (b) different orders may reach him at the same time and he does not know which he should carry out first.

Equally as bad as having two bosses is the situation where the supervisor is bypassed. Let us suppose you are a supervisor whose boss bypasses you (deals directly with people reporting to you). To the worker, it is the same as having two bosses; but to you, the supervisor, it is equally serious. Bypassing on the part of your boss will undermine your authority, and the people under you will begin looking to your boss for decisions and even for routine orders.

You can prevent bypassing by telling the people you supervise that if anyone tries to give them orders, they should direct that person to you.

II. SPAN OF CONTROL

Span of control on a given level involves:
A. The number of people being supervised
B. The distance
C. The time involved in supervising the people. (One supervisor cannot supervise too many workers effectively.)

Span of control means that a supervisor has the right number (not too many and not too few) of subordinates that he can supervise well.

III. UNIFORMITY OF ASSIGNMENT

In assigning work, you as the supervisor should assign to each person jobs that are similar in nature. An employee who is assigned too many different types of jobs will waste time in going from one kind of work to another. It takes time for him to get to top production in one kind of task and, before he does so, he has to start on another.
When you assign work to people, remember that:

A. Job duties should be definite. Make it clear from the beginning what they are to do, how they are to do it, and why they are to do it. Let them know how much they are expected to do and how well they are expected to do it.
B. Check your assignments to be certain that there are no workers with too many unrelated duties, and that no two people have been given overlapping responsibilities. Your aim should be to have every task assigned to a specific person with the work fairly distributed and with each person doing his part.

IV. ASSIGNMENT OF RESPONSIBILITY AND DELEGATION OF AUTHORITY

A supervisor cannot delegate his final responsibility for the work of his department. The experienced supervisor knows that he gets his work done through people. He can't do it all himself. So he must assign the work and the responsibility for the work to his employees. Then they must be given the authority to carry out their responsibilities.

By assigning responsibility and delegating authority to carry out the responsibility, the supervisor builds in his workers initiative, resourcefulness, enthusiasm, and interest in their work. He is treating them as responsible adults. They can find satisfaction in their work, and they will respect the supervisor and be loyal to the supervisor.

PRINCIPLES OF ORGANIZATION

I. DEFINITION

Organization is the method of dividing up the work to provide the best channels for coordinated effort to get the agency's mission accomplished.

II. PURPOSE OF ORGANIZATION

A. To enable each employee within the organization to clearly know his responsibilities and relationships to his fellow employees and to organizational units
B. To avoid conflicts of authority and overlapping of jurisdiction.
C. To ensure teamwork.

III. BASIC CONSIDERATIONS IIN ORGANIZATIONAL PLANNING

A. The basic plans and objectives of the agency should be determined, and the organizational structure should be adapted to carry out effectively such plans and objectives.
B. The organization should be built around the major functions of the agency and not individuals or groups of individuals.

C. The organization should be sufficiently flexible to meet new and changing conditions which may be brought about from within or outside the department.
D. The organizational structure should be as simple as possible and the number of organizational units kept at a minimum.
E. The number of levels of authority should be kept at a minimum. Each additional management level lengthens the chain of authority and responsibility and increases the time for instructions to be distributed to operating levels and for decisions to be obtained from higher authority.
F. The form of organization should permit each executive to exercise maximum initiative within the limits of delegated authority.

IV. BASES FOR ORGANIZATION

A. Purpose (Examples: education, police, sanitation)
B. Process (Examples: accounting, legal, purchasing)
C. Clientele (Examples: welfare, parks, veteran)
D. Geographic (Examples: borough offices, precincts, libraries)

V. ASSIGNMENTS OF FUNCTIONS

A. Every function of the agency should be assigned to a specific organizational unit. Under normal circumstances, no single function should be assigned to more than one organizational unit.
B. There should be no overlapping, duplication, or conflict between organizational elements.
C. Line functions should be separated from staff functions, and proper emphasis should be placed on staff activities.
D. Functions which are closely related or similar should normally be assigned to a single organizational unit.
E. Functions should be properly distributed to promote balance, and to avoid overemphasis of less important functions and underemphasis of more essential functions.

VI. DELEGATION OF AUTHORITY AND RESPONSIBILITY

A. Responsibilities assigned to a specific individual or organizational unit should carry corresponding authority, and all statements of authority or limitations thereof should be as specific as possible.
B. Authority and responsibility for action should be decentralized to organizational units and individuals responsible for actual performance to the greatest extent possible, without relaxing necessary control over policy or the standardization of procedures. Delegation of authority will be consistent with decentralization of responsibility but such delegation will not divest an executive in higher authority of his overall responsibility.
C. The heads of organizational units should concern themselves with important matters and should delegate to the maximum extent details and routines performed in the ordinary course of business.
D. All responsibilities, authorities, and relationships should be stated in simple language to avoid misinterpretation.
E. Each individual or organizational unit charged with a specific responsibility will be held responsible for results.

VII. EMPLOYEE RELATIONSHIPS

   A. The employees reporting to one executive should not exceed the number which can be effectively directed and coordinated. The number will depend largely upon the scope and extent of the responsibilities of the subordinates.
   B. No person should report to more than one supervisor. Every supervisor should know who reports to him, and every employee should know to whom he reports. Channels of authority and responsibility should not be violated by staff units.
   C. Relationships between organizational units within the agency and with outside organizations and associations should be clearly stated and thoroughly understood to avoid misunderstanding.

DELEGATING

I. WHAT IS DELEGATING?
Delegating is assigning a job to an employee, giving him the authority to get that job done, and giving him the responsibility for seeing to it that the job is done.

   A. What To Delegate
      1. Routine details
      2. Jobs which may be necessary and take a lot of time, but do not have to be done by the supervisor personally (preparing reports, attending meetings, etc.)
      3. Routine decision-making (making decisions which do not require the supervisor's personal attention)

   B. What Not To Delegate
      1. Job details which are *executive functions* (setting goals, organizing employees into a good team, analyzing results so as to plan for the future)
      2. Disciplinary power (handling grievances, preparing service ratings, reprimands, etc.)
      3. Decision-making which involves large numbers of employees or other bureaus and departments
      4. Final and complete responsibility for the job done by the unit being supervised

   C. Why Delegate?
      1. To strengthen the organization by developing a greater number of skilled employees
      2. To improve the employee's performance by giving him the chance to learn more about the job, handle some responsibility, and become more interested in getting the job done
      3. To improve a supervisor's performance by relieving him of routine jobs and giving him more time for *executive functions* (planning, organizing, controlling, etc.) which cannot be delegated

II. TO WHOM TO DELEGATE
People with abilities not being used. Selection should be based on ability, not on favoritism.

REPORTS

I. DEFINITION
A report is an orderly presentation of factual information directed to a specific reader for a specific purpose

II. PURPOSE
The general purpose of a report is to bring to the reader useful and factual information about a condition or a problem. Some specific purposes of a report may be:

  A. To enable the reader to appraise the efficiency or effectiveness of a person or an operation
  B. To provide a basis for establishing standards
  C. To reflect the results of expenditures of time, effort, and money
  D. To provide a basis for developing or altering programs

III. TYPES

  A. Information Report: Contains facts arranged in sequence
  B. Summary (Examination) Report: Contains facts plus an analysis or discussion of the significance of the facts. Analysis may give advantages and disadvantages or give qualitative and quantitative comparisons
  C. Recommendation Report: Contains facts, analysis, and conclusion logically drawn from the facts and analysis, plus a recommendation based upon the facts, analysis, and conclusions

IV. FACTORS TO CONSIDER BEFORE WRITING REPORT

  A. <u>Why</u> write the report?: The purpose of the report should be clearly defined.
  B. <u>Who</u> will read the report?: What level of language should be used? Will the reader understand professional or technical language?
  C. <u>What</u> should be said?: What does the reader need or want to know about the subject?
  D. <u>How</u> should it be said?: Should the subject be presented tactfully? Convincingly? In a stimulating manner?

V. PREPARATORY STEPS

  A. Assemble the facts: Find out who, why, what, where, when, and how.
  B. Organize the facts: Eliminate unnecessary information
  C. Prepare an outline: Check for orderliness, logical sequence
  D. Prepare a draft: Check for correctness, clearness, completeness, conciseness, and tone
  E. Prepare it in final form: Check for grammar, punctuation, appearance

VI. OUTLINE FOR A RECOMMENDATION REPORT

  Is the report:
  A. Correct in information, grammar, and tone?
  B. Clear?
  C. Complete?

D. Concise?
E. Timely?
F. Worth its cost?

Will the report accomplish its purpose?

MANAGEMENT CONTROLS

I. CONTROL

What is control? What is controlled? Who controls?

The essence of control is action which adjusts operations to predetermined standards, and its basis is information in the hands of managers. Control is checking to determine whether plans are being observed and suitable progress toward stated objectives is being made, and action is taken, if necessary, to correct deviations.

We have a ready-made model for this concept of control in the automatic systems which are widely used for process control in the chemical land petroleum industries. A process control system works this way. Suppose, for example, it is desired to maintain a constant rate of flow of oil through a pipe at a predetermined or set-point value. A signal, whose strength represents the rate of flow, can be produced in a measuring device and transmitted to a control mechanism. The control mechanism, when it detects any deviation of the actual from the set-point signal, will reposition the value regulating flow rate.

II. BASIS FOR CONTROL

A process control mechanism thus acts to adjust operations to predetermined standards and does so on the basis of information it receives. In a parallel way, information reaching a manager gives him the opportunity for corrective action and is his basis for control. He cannot exercise control without such information, and he cannot do a complete job of managing without controlling.

III. POLICY

What is policy?

Policy is simply a statement of an organization's intention to act in certain ways when specified types of circumstances arise. It represents a general decision, predetermined and expressed as a principle or rule, establishing a normal pattern of conduct for dealing with given types of business events—usually recurrent. A statement is therefore useful in economizing the time of managers and in assisting them to discharge their responsibilities equitably and consistently.

Policy is not a means of control, but policy does generate the need for control.

Adherence to policies is not guaranteed nor can it be taken on faith. It has to be verified. Without verification, there is no basis for control. Policy and procedures, although closely related and interdependent to a certain extent, are not synonymous. A policy may be adopted, for example, to maintain a materials inventory not to exceed one million dollars.

A procedure for inventory control could interpret that policy and convert it into methods for keeping within that limit, with consideration, too, of possible but foreseeable expedient deviation.

IV. PROCEDURE

What is procedure?

A procedure specifically prescribes:
A. What work is to be performed by the various participants
B. Who are the respective participants
C. When and where the various steps in the different processes are to be performed
D. The sequence of operations that will insure uniform handling of recurring transactions
E. The paper that is involved, its origin, transition, and disposition

Necessary appurtenances to a procedure are:
A. Detailed organizational chart
B. Flow charts
C. Exhibits of forms, all presented in close proximity to the text of the procedure

V. BASIS OF CONTROL – INFORMATION IN THE HANDS OF MANAGERS

If the basis of control is information in the hands of managers, then reporting is elevated to a level of very considerable importance.

Types of reporting may include:
A. Special reports and routine reports
B. Written, oral, and graphic reports
C. Staff meetings
D. Conferences
E. Television screens
F. Non-receipt of information, as where management is by exception
G. Any other means whereby information is transmitted to a manager as a basis for control action

FRAMEWORK OF MANAGEMENT

I. ELEMENTS

A. Policy: It has to be verified, controlled.

B. Organization is part of the giving of an assignment. The organizational chart gives to each individual in his title, a first approximation of the nature of his assignment and orients him as being accountable to a certain individual. Organization is not in a true sense a means of control. Control is checking to ascertain whether the assignment is executed as intended and acting on the basis of that information.

C. Budgets perform three functions:
1. They present the objectives, plans, and programs of the organization in financial terms.

2. They report the progress of actual performance against these predetermined objectives, plans, and programs.
3. Like organizational charts, delegations of authority, procedures, and job descriptions, they define the assignments which have flowed from the Chief Executive. Budgets are a means of control in the respect that they report progress of actual performance against the program. They provide information which enables managers to take action directed toward bringing actual results into conformity with the program.

D. Internal Check provides in practice for the principle that the same person should not have responsibility for all phases of a transaction. This makes it clearly an aspect of organization rather than of control. Internal Check is static, or built-in.

E. Plans, Programs, Objectives
People must know what they are trying to do. Objectives fulfill this need. Without them, people may work industriously and yet, working aimlessly, accomplish little. Plans and Programs complement Objectives, since they propose how and according to what time schedule the objectives are to be reached.

F. Delegations of Authority
Among the ways we have for supplementing the titles and lines of authority of an organizational chart are delegations of authority. Delegations of authority clarify the extent of authority of individuals and in that way serve to define assignments. That they are not means of control is apparent from the very fact that wherever there has been a delegation of authority, the need for control increases. This could hardly be expected to happen if delegations of authority were themselves means of control.

II. MANAGER'S RESPONSIBILITY

Control becomes necessary whenever a manager delegates authority to a subordinate because he cannot delegate and then simply sit back and forget4 about it. A manager's accountability to his own superior has not diminished one whit as a result of delegating part of his authority to a subordinate. The manager must exercise control over actions taken under the authority so delegated. That means checking serves as a basis for possible corrective action.

Objectives, plans, programs, organizational charts, and other elements of the managerial system are not fruitfully regarded as either controls or means of control. They are pre-established standards or models of performance to which operations are adjusted by the exercise of management control. These standards or models of performance are dynamic in character for they are constantly altered, modified, or revised. Policies, organizational set-up, procedures, delegations, etc. are constantly altered but, like objectives and plans, they remain in force until they are either abandoned or revised. All of the elements (or standards or models of performance), objectives, plans, and programs, policies, organization, etc. can be regarded as a *framework of management*.

III. CONTROL TECHNIQUES

Examples of control techniques:
A. Compare against established standards
B. Compare with a similar operation
C. Compare with past operations
D. Compare with predictions of accomplishment

IV. WHERE FORECASTS FIT

Control is after-the-fact while forecasts are before. Forecasts and projections are important for setting objectives and formulating plans.

Information for aiming and planning does not have to be before-the-fact. It may be an after-the-fact analysis proving that a certain policy has been impolitic in its effect on the relation of the company or department with customer, employee, taxpayer, or stockholder; or that a certain plan is no longer practical, or that a certain procedure is unworkable.

The prescription here certainly would not be in control (in these cases, control would simply bring operations into conformity with obsolete standards) but the establishment of new standards, a new policy, a new plan, and a new procedure to be controlled too.

Information is, of course, the basis for all communication in addition to furnishing evidence to management of the need for reconstructing the framework of management.

PROBLEM SOLVING

The accepted concept in modern management for problem solving is the utilization of the following steps:

A. Identify the problem
B. Gather data
C. List possible solutions
D. Test possible solutions
E. Select the best solution
F. Put the solution into actual practice

Occasions might arise where you would have to apply the second step of gathering data before completing the first step.

You might also find that it will be necessary to work on several steps at the same time.

I. IDENTIFY THE PROBLEM

Your first step is to define as precisely as possible the problem to be solved. While this may sound easy, it is often the most difficult part of the process.

It has been said of problem solving that you are halfway to the solution when you can write out a clear statement of the problem itself.

Our job now is to get below the surface manifestations of the trouble and pinpoint the problem. This is usually accomplished by a logical analysis, by going from the general to the particular; from the obvious to the not-so-obvious cause.

Let us say that production is behind schedule. WHY? Absenteeism is high. Now, is absenteeism the basic problem to be tackled, or is it merely a symptom of low morale among the workforce? Under these circumstances, you may decide that production is not the problem; the problem is *employee morale*.

In trying to define the problem, remember there is seldom one simple reason why production is lagging, or reports are late, etc.

Analysis usually leads to the discovery that an apparent problem is really made up of several subproblems which must be attacked separately.

Another way is to limit the problem, and thereby ease the task of finding a solution, and concentrate on the elements which are within the scope of your control.

When you have gone this far, write out a tentative statement of the problem to be solved.

II. GATHER DATA

In the second step, you must set out to collect all the information that might have a bearing on the problem. Do not settle for an assumption when reasonable fact and figures are available.

If you merely go through the motions of problem-solving, you will probably shortcut the information-gathering step. Therefore, do not stack the evidence by confining your research to your own preconceived ideas.

As you collect facts, organize them in some form that helps you make sense of them and spot possible relationships between them. For example, plotting cost per unit figures on a graph can be more meaningful than a long column of figures.

Evaluate each item as you go along. Is the source material absolutely, reliable, probably reliable, or not to be trusted.

One of the best methods for gathering data is to go out and look the situation over carefully. Talk to the people on the job who are most affected by this problem.

Always keep in mind that a primary source is usually better than a secondary source of information.

III. LIST POSSIBLE SOLUTIONS

This is the creative thinking step of problem solving. This is a good time to bring into play whatever techniques of group dynamics the agency or bureau might have developed for a joint attack on problems.

Now the important thing for you to do is: Keep an open mind. Let your imagination roam freely over the facts you have collected. Jot down every possible solution that occurs to you. Resist the temptation to evaluate various proposals as you go along. List seemingly absurd ideas along with more plausible ones. The more possibilities you list during this step, the less risk you will run of settling for merely a workable, rather than the best, solution.

Keep studying the data as long as there seems to be any chance of deriving additional ideas, solutions, explanations, or patterns from it.

IV. TEST POSSIBLE SOLUTIONS

Now you begin to evaluate the possible solutions. Take pains to be objective. Up to this point, you have suspended judgment but you might be tempted to select a solution you secretly favored all along and proclaim it as the best of the lot.

The secret of objectivity in this phase is to test the possible solutions separately, measuring each against a common yardstick. To make this yardstick try to enumerate as many specific criteria as you can think of. Criteria are best phrased as questions which you ask of each possible solution. They can be drawn from these general categories:

- Suitability – Will this solution do the job?
  Will it solve the problem completely or partially?
  Is it a permanent or a stopgap solution?

- Feasibility - Will this plan work in actual practice?
  Can we afford this approach?
  How much will it cost?

- Acceptability - Will the boss go along with the changes required in the plan?
  Are we trying to drive a tack with a sledge hammer?

V. SELECT THE BEST SOLUTION

This is the area of executive decision.

Occasionally, one clearly superior solution will stand out at the conclusion of the testing process. But often it is not that simple. You may find that no one solution has come through all the tests with flying colors.

You may also find that a proposal, which flunked miserably on one of the essential tests, racked up a very high score on others.

The best solution frequently will turn out to be a combination.

Try to arrange a marriage that will bring together the strong points of one possible solution with the particular virtues of another. The more skill and imagination that you apply, the greater is the likelihood that you will come out with a solution that is not merely adequate and workable, but is the best possible under the circumstances.

VI. PUT THE SOLUTION INTO ACTUAL PRACTICE

As every executive knows, a plan which works perfectly on paper may develop all sorts of bugs when put into actual practice.

Problem-solving does not stop with selecting the solution which looks best in theory. The next step is to put the chosen solution into action and watch the results. The results may point towards modifications.

If the problem disappears when you put your solution into effect, you know you have the right solution.

If it does not disappear, even after you have adjusted your plan to cover unforeseen difficulties that turned up in practice, work your way back through the problem-solving solutions.

> Would one of them have worked better?
> Did you overlook some vital piece of data which would have given you a different slant on the whole situation? Did you apply all necessary criteria in testing solutions? If no light dawns after this much rechecking, it is a pretty good bet that you defined the problem incorrectly in the first place.

You came up with the wrong solution because you tackled the wrong problem.

Thus, step six may become step one of a new problem-solving cycle.

COMMUNICATION

I. WHAT IS COMMUNICATION?
We communicate through writing, speaking, action, or inaction. In speaking to people face-to-face, there is opportunity to judge reactions and to adjust the message. This makes the supervisory chain one of the most, and in many instances the most, important channels of communication.

In an organization, communication means keeping employees informed about the organization's objectives, policies, problems, and progress. Communication is the free interchange of information, ideas, and desirable attitudes between and among employees and between employees and management.

II. WHY IS COMMUNICATION NEEDED?

   A. People have certain social needs
   B. Good communication is essential in meeting those social needs
   C. While people have similar basic needs, at the same time they differ from each other
   D. Communication must be adapted to these individual differences

An employee cannot do his best work unless he knows why he is doing it. If he has the feeling that he is being kept in the dark about what is going on, his enthusiasm and productivity suffer.

Effective communication is needed in an organization so that employees will understand what the organization is trying to accomplish; and how the work of one unit contributes to or affects the work of other units in the organization and other organizations.

III. HOW IS COMMUNICATION ACHIEVED?

Communication flows downward, upward, sideways.

A. Communication may come from top management down to employees. This is downward communication.

  Some means of downward communication are:
  1. Training (orientation, job instruction, supervision, public relations, etc.)
  2. Conferences
  3. Staff meetings
  4. Policy statements
  5. Bulletins
  6. Newsletters
  7. Memoranda
  8. Circulation of important letters

  In downward communication, it is important that employees be informed in advance of changes that will affect them.

B. Communications should also be developed so that the ideas, suggestions, and knowledge of employees will flow upward to top management.

  Some means of upward communication are:
  1. Personal discussion conferences
  2. Committees
  3. Memoranda
  4. Employees suggestion program
  5. Questionnaires to be filled in giving comments and suggestions about proposed actions that will affect field operations.

  Upward communication requires that management be willing to listen, to accept, and to make changes when good ideas are present. Upward communication succeeds when there is no fear of punishment for speaking out or lack of interest at the top. Employees will share their knowledge and ideas with management when interest is shown and recognition is given.

C. The advantages of downward communication:
  1. It enables the passing down of orders, policies, and plans necessary to the continued operation of the station.
  2. By making information available, it diminishes the fears and suspicions which result from misinformation and misunderstanding.
  3. It fosters the pride people want to have in their work when they are told of good work.
  4. It improves the morale and stature of the individual to be *in the know.*

5. It helps employees to understand, accept, and cooperate with changes when they know about them in advance.

D. The advantages of upward communication:
1. It enables the passing upward of information, attitudes, and feelings.
2. It makes it easier to find out how ready people are to receive downward communication.
3. It reveals the degree to which the downward communication is understood and accepted.
4. It helps to satisfy the basic social needs.
5. It stimulates employees to participate in the operation of their organization.
6. It encourage employees to contribute ideas for improving the efficiency and economy of operations.
7. It helps to solve problem situations before they reach the explosion point.

IV. WHY DOES COMMUNICATION FAIL?

A. The technical difficulties of conveying information clearly
B. The emotional content of communication which prevents complete transmission
C. The fact that there is a difference between what management needs to say, what it wants to day, and what it does say
D. The fact that there is a difference between what employees would like to say, what they think is profitable or safe to say, and what they do say

V. HOW TO IMPROVE COMMUNICATION

As a supervisor, you are a key figure in communication. To improve as a communicator, you should:
A. Know: Knowing your subordinates will help you to recognize and work with individual differences.
B. Like: If you like those who work for you and those for whom you work, this will foster the kind of friendly, warm, work atmosphere that will facilitate communication.
C. Trust: Showing a sincere desire to communicate will help to develop the mutual trust and confidence which are essential to the free flow of communication.
D. Tell: Tell your subordinates and superiors *what's doing*. Tell your subordinates *why* as well as *how*.
E. Listen: By listening, you help others to talk and you create good listeners. Don't forget that listening implies action.
F. Stimulate: Communication has to be stimulated and encouraged. Be receptive to ideas and suggestions and motivate your people so that each member of the team identifies himself with the job at hand.
G. Consult: The most effective way of consulting is to let your people participate, insofar as possible, in developing determinations which affect them or their work.

VI. HOW TO DETERMINE WHETHER YOU ARE GETTING ACROSS

A. Check to see that communication is received and understood
B. Judge this understanding by actions rather than words
C. Adapt or vary communication, when necessary
D. Remember that good communication cannot cure all problems

VII. THE KEY ATTITUDE

Try to see things from the other person's point of view. By doing this, you help to develop the permissive atmosphere and the shared confidence and understanding which are essential to effective two-way communication.

Communication is a two-way process:
A. The basic purpose of any communication is to get action.
B. The only way to get action is through acceptance.
C. In order to get acceptance, communication must be humanly satisfying as well as technically efficient.

HOW ORDERS AND INSTRUCTIONS SHOULD BE GIVEN

I. CHARACTERISTICS OF GOOD ORDERS AND INSTRUCTIONS

   A. Clear
      Orders should be definite as to
      —What is to be done
      —Who is to do it
      —When it is to be done
      —Where it is to be done
      —How it is to be done

   B. Concise
      Avoid wordiness. Orders should be brief and to the point.

   C. Timely
      Instructions and orders should be sent out at the proper time and not too long in advance of expected performance.

   D. Possibility of Performance
      Orders should be feasible:
      1. Investigate before giving orders
      2. Consult those who are to carry out instructions before formulating and issuing them

   E. Properly Directed
      Give the orders to the people concerned. Do not send orders to people who are not concerned. People who continually receive instructions that are not applicable to them get in the habit of neglecting instructions generally.

   F. Reviewed Before Issuance
      Orders should be reviewed before issuance:
      1. Test them by putting yourself in the position of the recipient
      2. If they involve new procedures, have the persons who are to do the work review them for suggestions.

   G. Reviewed After Issuance
      Persons who receive orders should be allowed to raise questions and to point out unforeseen consequences of orders.

H. Coordinated
Orders should be coordinated so that work runs smoothly.

I. Courteous
Make a request rather than a demand. There is no need to continually call attention to the fact that you are the boss.

J. Recognizable as an Order
Be sure that the order is recognizable as such.

K. Complete
Be sure recipient has knowledge and experience sufficient to carry out order. Give illustrations and examples.

A DEPARTMENTAL PERSONNEL OFFICE IS RESPONSIBLE FOR THE FOLLOWING FUNCTIONS

1. Policy
2. Personnel Programs
3. Recruitment and Placement
4. Position Classification
5. Salary and Wage Administration
6. Employee performance Standards and Evaluation
7. Employee Relations
8. Disciplinary Actions and Separations
9. Health and Safety
10. Staff Training and Development
11. Personnel Records, Procedures, and Reports
12. Employee Services
13. Personnel Research

SUPERVISION

I. LEADERSHIP

All leadership is based essentially on authority. This comes from two sources: It is received from higher management or it is earned by the supervisor through his methods of supervision. Although effective leadership has always depended upon the leader's using his authority in such a way as to appeal successfully to the motives of the people supervised, the conditions for making this appeal are continually changing. The key to today's problem of leadership is flexibility and resourcefulness on the part of the leader in meeting changes in conditions as they occur.

Three basic approaches to leadership are generally recognized:

A. The Authoritarian Approach
   1. The methods and techniques used in this approach emphasize the / in leadership and depend primarily on the formal authority of the leader. This authority is sometimes exercised in a hardboiled manner and sometimes in a benevolent

manner, but in either case the dominating role of the leader is reflected in the thinking, planning, and decisions of the group.
2. Group results are to a large degree dependent on close supervision by the leader. Usually, the individuals in the group will not show a high degree of initiative or acceptance of responsibility and their capacity to grow and develop probably will not be fully utilized. The group may react with resentment or submission, depending upon the manner and skill of the leader in using his authority.
3. This approach develops as a natural outgrowth of the authority that goes with the leader's job and his feeling of sole responsibility for getting the job done. It is relatively easy to use and does not require must resourcefulness.
4. The use of this approach is effective in times of emergencies, in meeting close deadline as a final resort, in settling some issues, in disciplinary matters, and with dependent individuals and groups.

B. The Laissez-Faire or Let 'em Alone Approach
1. This approach generally is characterized by an avoidance of leadership responsibility by the leader. The activities of the group depend largely on the choice of its members rather than the leader.
2. Group results probably will be poor. Generally, there will be disagreements over petty things, bickering, and confusion. Except for a few aggressive people, individuals will not show much initiative and growth and development will be retarded. There may be a tendency for informal leaders to take over leadership of the group.
3. This approach frequently results from the leader's dislike of responsibility, from his lack of confidence, from failure of other methods to work, from disappointment or criticism. It is usually the easiest of the three to use and requires both understanding and resourcefulness on the part of the leader.
4. This approach is occasionally useful and effective, particularly in forcing dependent individuals or groups to rely on themselves, to give someone a chance to save face by clearing his own difficulties, or when action should be delayed temporarily for good cause.

C. The Democratic Approach
1. The methods and techniques used in this approach emphasize the *we* in leadership and build up the responsibility of the group to attain its objectives. Reliance is placed largely on the earned authority of the leader.
2. Group results are likely to be good because most of the job motives of the people will be satisfied. Cooperation and teamwork, initiative, acceptance of responsibility, and the individual's capacity for growth probably will show a high degree of development.
3. This approach grows out of a desire or necessity of the leader to find ways to appeal effectively to the motivation of his group. It is the best approach to build up inside the person a strong desire to cooperate and apply himself to the job. It is the most difficult to develop, and requires both understanding and resourcefulness on the part of the leader.
4. The value of this approach increases over a long period where sustained efficiency and development of people are important. It may not be fully effective in all situations, however, particularly when there is not sufficient time to use it properly or where quick decisions must be made.

All three approaches are used by most leaders and have a place in supervising people. The extent of their use varies with individual leaders, with some using one approach predominantly. The leader who uses these three approaches, and varies their use with time and circumstance, is probably the most effective. Leadership which is used predominantly with a democratic approach requires more resourcefulness on the part of the leader but offers the greatest possibilities in terms of teamwork and cooperation.

The one best way of developing democratic leadership is to provide a real sense of participation on the part of the group, since this satisfies most of the chief job motives. Although there are many ways of providing participation, consulting as frequently as possible with individuals and groups on things that affect them seems to offer the most in building cooperation and responsibility. Consultation takes different forms, but it is most constructive when people feel they are actually helping in finding the answers to the problems on the job.

There are some requirements of leaders in respect to human relations which should be considered in their selection and development. Generally, the leader should be interested in working with other people, emotionally stable, self-confident, and sensitive to the reactions of others. In addition, his viewpoint should be one of getting the job done through people who work cooperatively in response to his leadership. He should have a knowledge of individual and group behavior, but, most important of all, he should work to combine all of these requirements into a definite, practical skill in leadership.

II. NINE POINTS OF CONTRAST BETWEEN *BOSS* AND *LEADER*

   A. The boss drives his men; the leader coaches them.
   B. The boss depends on authority; the leader on good will.
   C. The boss inspires fear; the leader inspires enthusiasm.
   D. The boss says I; the leader says *We*.
   E. The boss says *Get here on time*; the leader gets there ahead of time.
   F. The boss fixes the blame for the breakdown; the leader fixes the breakdown.
   G. The boss knows how it is done; the leader shows how.
   H. The boss makes work a drudgery; the leader makes work a game.
   I. The boss says *Go*; the leader says *Let's go*.

EMPLOYEE MORALE

Employee morale is the way employees feel about each other, the organization or unit in which they work, and the work they perform.

I. SOME WAYS TO DEVELOP AND MAINTAIN GOOD EMPLYEE MORALE

   A. Give adequate credit and praise when due.
   B. Recognize importance of all jobs and equalize load with proper assignments, always giving consideration to personality differences and abilities.
   C. Welcome suggestions and do not have an *all-wise* attitude. Request employees' assistance in solving problems and use assistants when conducting group meetings on certain subjects.
   D. Properly assign responsibilities and give adequate authority for fulfillment of such assignments.

E. Keep employees informed about matters that affect them.
F. Criticize and reprimand employees privately.
G. Be accessible and willing to listen.
H. Be fair.
I. Be alert to detect training possibilities so that you will not miss an opportunity to help each employee do a better job, and if possible with less effort on his part.
J. Set a good example.
K. Apply the golden rule.

II. SOME INDICATIONS OF GOOD MORALE

A. Good quality of work
B. Good quantity
C. Good attitude of employees
D. Good discipline
E. Teamwork
F. Good attendance
G. Employee participation

MOTIVATION

DRIVES

A drive, stated simply, is a desire or force which causes a person to do or say certain things. These are some of the most usual drives and some of their identifying characteristics recognizable in people motivated by such drives:

A. Security (desire to provide for the future)
   Always on time for work
   Works for the same employer for many years
   Never takes unnecessary chances
   Seldom resists doing what he is told

B. Recognition (desire to be rewarded for accomplishment)
   Likes to be asked for his opinion
   Becomes very disturbed when he makes a mistake
   Does things to attract attention
   Likes to see his name in print

C. Position (desire to hold certain status in relation to others)
   Boasts about important people he knows
   Wants to be known as a key man
   Likes titles
   Demands respect
   Belongs to clubs, for prestige

D. Accomplishment (desire to get things done)
   Complains when things are held up
   Likes to do things that have tangible results
   Never lies down on the job
   Is proud of turning out good work

E. Companionship (desire to associate with other people)
   Likes to work with others
   Tells stories and jokes
   Indulges in horseplay
   Finds excuses to talk to others on the job

F. Possession (desire to collect and hoard objects)
   Likes to collect things
   Puts his name on things belonging to him
   Insists on the same location

Supervisors may find that identifying the drives of employees is a helpful step toward motivating them to self-improvement and better job performance. For example: An employee's job performance is below average. His supervisor, having previously determined that the employee is motivated by a drive for security, suggests that taking training courses will help the employee to improve, advance, and earn more money. Since earning more money can be a step toward greater security, the employee's drive for security would motivate him to take the training suggested by the supervisor. In essence, this is the process of charting an employee's future course by using his motivating drives to positive advantage.

EMPLOYEE PARTICIPATION

I. WHAT IS PARTICIPATION

Employee participation is the employee's giving freely of his time, skill, and knowledge to an extent which cannot be obtained by demand.

II. WHY IS IT IMPORTANT?

The supervisor's responsibility is to get the job done through people. A good supervisor gets the job done through people who work willingly and well. The participation of employees is important because:

A. Employees develop a greater sense of responsibility when they share in working out operating plans and goals.
B. Participation provides greater opportunity and stimulation for employees to learn, and to develop their ability.
C. Participation sometimes provides better solutions to problems because such solutions may combine the experience and knowledge of interested employees who want the solutions to work.
D. An employee or group may offer a solution which the supervisor might hesitate to make for fear of demanding too much.

E. Since the group wants to make the solution work, they exert pressure in a constructive way on each other.
F. Participation usually results in reducing the need for close supervision.

II. HOW MAY SUPERVISORS OBTAIN IT?

Participation is encouraged when employees feel that they share some responsibility for the work and that their ideas are sincerely wanted and valued. Some ways of obtaining employee participation are:

A. Conduct orientation programs for new employees to inform them about the organization and their rights and responsibilities as employees.
B. Explain the aims and objectives of the agency. On a continuing basis, be sure that the employees know what these aims and objectives are.
C. Share job successes and responsibilities and give credit for success.
D. Consult with employees, both as individuals and in groups, about things that affect them.
E. Encourage suggestions for job improvements. Help employees to develop good suggestions. The suggestions can bring them recognition. The city's suggestion program offers additional encouragement through cash awards.

The supervisor who encourages employee participation is not surrendering his authority. He must still make decisions and initiate action, and he must continue to be ultimately responsible for the work of those he supervises. But, through employee participation, he is helping his group to develop greater ability and a sense of responsibility while getting the job done faster and better.

STEPS IN HANDLING A GRIEVANCE

1. Get the Facts
    a. Listen sympathetically
    b. Let him talk himself out
    c. Get his story straight
    d. Get his point of view
    e. Don't argue with him
    f. Give him plenty of time
    g. Conduct the interview privately
    h. Don't try to shift the blame or pass the buck

2. Consider the Facts
    a. Consider the employee's viewpoint
    b. How will the decision affect similar cases
    c. Consider each decision as a possible precedent
    d. Avoid snap judgments—don't jump to conclusions

3. Make or Get a Decision
    a. Frame an effective counter-proposal
    b. Make sure it is fair to all
    c. Have confidence in your judgment
    d. Be sure you can substantiate your decision

4. Notify the Employee of Your Decision
   Be sure he is told; try to convince him that the decision is fair and just.

5. Take Action When Needed and If Within Your Authority
   Otherwise, tell employee that the matter will be called to the attention of the proper person or that nothing can be done, and why it cannot.

6. Follow through to see that the desired result is achieved.

7. Record key facts concerning the complaint and the action taken.

8. Leave the way open to him to appeal your decision to a higher authority.

9. Report all grievances to your superior, whether they are appealed or not.

DISCIPLINE

Discipline is training that develops self-control, orderly conduct, and efficiency.

To discipline does not necessarily mean to punish.

To discipline does mean to train, to regulate, and to govern conduct.

I. THE DISCIPLINARY INTERVIEW

Most employees sincerely want to do what is expected of them. In other words, they are self-disciplined. Some employees, however, fail to observe established rules and standards, and disciplinary action by the supervisor is required.

The primary purpose of disciplinary action is to improve conduct without creating dissatisfaction, bitterness, or resentment in the process.

Constructive disciplinary action is more concerned with causes and explanations of breaches of conduct than with punishment. The disciplinary interview is held to get at the causes of apparent misbehavior and to motivate better performance in the future.

It is important that the interview be kept on an impersonal a basis as possible. If the supervisor lets the interview descend to the plane of an argument, it loses its effectiveness.

II. PLANNING THE INTERVIEW

Get all pertinent facts concerning the situation so that you can talk in specific terms to the employee.

Review the employee's record, appraisal ratings, etc.

Consider what you know about the temperament of the employee. Consider your attitude toward the employee. Remember that the primary requisite of disciplinary action is fairness.

Don't enter upon the interview when angry.

Schedule the interview for a place which is private and out of hearing of others.

III. CONDUCTING THE INTERVIEW

A. Make an effort to establish accord.
B. Question the employee about the apparent breach of discipline. Be sure that the question is not so worded as to be itself an accusation.
C. Give the employee a chance to tell his side of the story. Give him ample opportunity to talk.
D. Use understanding—listening except where it is necessary to ask a question or to point out some details of which the employee may not be aware. If the employee misrepresents facts, make a plain, accurate statement of the facts, but don't argue and don't engage in personal controversy.
E. Listen and try to understand the reasons for the employee's (mis)conduct. First of all, don't assume that there has been a breach of discipline. Evaluate the employee's reasons for his conduct in the light of his opinions and feelings concerning the consistency and reasonableness of the standards which he was expected to follow. Has the supervisor done his part in explaining the reasons for the rule? Was the employee's behavior unintentional or deliberate? Does he think he had real reasons for his actions? What new facts is he telling? Do the facts justify his actions? What causes, other than those mentioned, could have stimulated the behavior?
F. After listening to the employee's version of the situation, and if censure of his actions is warranted, the supervisor should proceed with whatever criticism is justified. Emphasis should be placed on future improvement rather than exclusively on the employee's failure to measure up to expected standards of job conduct.
G. Fit the criticism to the individual. With one employee, a word of correction may be all that is required.
H. Attempt to distinguish between unintentional error and deliberate misbehavior. An error due to ignorance requires training and not censure.
I. Administer criticism in a controlled, even tone of voice, never in anger. Make it clear that you are acting as an agent of the department. In general, criticism should refer to the job or the employee's actions and not to the person. Criticism of the employee's work is not an attack on the individual.
J. Be sure the interview does not destroy the employee's self-confidence. Mention his good qualities and assure him that you feel confident that he can improve his performance.
K. Wherever possible, before the employee leaves the interview, satisfy him that the incident is closed, that nothing more will be said on the subject unless the offense is repeated.

www.ingramcontent.com/pod-product-compliance
Lightning Source LLC
Chambersburg PA
CBHW081811300426
44116CB00014B/2312